Be Your Own Financial Advisor

Robert E. Pritchard
Gregory C. Potter
Larry E. Howe

Glassboro State College

PRENTICE HALL, ENGLEWOOD CLIFFS, NEW JERSEY 07632

Library of Congress Cataloging-in-Publication Data

PRITCHARD, ROBERT E. (DATE)
   Be your own financial advisor.
    Includes index.
    1. Finance, Personal—United States. 2. Investments—United States. I. Potter, Gregory C. II. Howe, Larry E. III. Title.
HG179.P737   1988   332.024   87–14366
ISBN 0-13-071242-6

Editorial/production supervision
and interior design: *Gloria L. Jordan*
Cover design: *Photo Plus Art*
Manufacturing buyer: *Lorraine Fumoso*

The publisher offers discounts on this book when ordered in bulk quantities. For more information, write:
Special Sales/College Marketing
Prentice Hall
College Technical and Reference Division
Englewood Cliffs, N.J. 07632

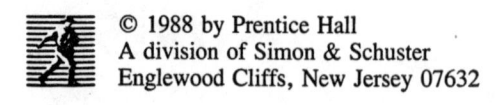

© 1988 by Prentice Hall
A division of Simon & Schuster
Englewood Cliffs, New Jersey 07632

All rights reserved. No part of this book may be
reproduced, in any form or by any means,
without permission in writing from the publisher.

Printed in the United States of America
10 9 8 7 6 5 4 3 2 1

ISBN 0-13-071242-6 025

Prentice Hall International (UK) Limited, *London*
Prentice Hall of Australia Pty. Limited, *Sydney*
Prentice Hall Canada Inc., *Toronto*
Prentice Hall Hispanoamericana, S.A., *Mexico*
Prentice Hall of India Private Limited, *New Delhi*
Prentice Hall of Japan, Inc., *Tokyo*
Simon & Schuster Asia Pte. Ltd., *Singapore*
Editora Prentice Hall do Brasil, Ltda., *Rio de Janeiro*

*For Carol,
Sodie,
and Pat*

Contents

PREFACE   IX

ACKNOWLEDGMENTS   XIII

1 KEEPING THE HORSE AHEAD OF THE CART   1

Managing Your Money and Employee Fringe Benefits   *5*
Home Equity Loans   *10*
Establishing Financial Goals   *12*
Some Basics about Interest   *14*
Compound Interest—the Eighth Wonder of the World   *15*
Capitalizing on Compound Interest   *18*
Basics of Investments—Starting Your Investment Program   *18*

2 THERE'S NO PLACE LIKE HOME   21

Five Good Reasons to Own a Home   *23*
Should Everyone Own a Home?   *24*
The Best Home for You   *25*
Finding a Good Location   *28*
Buying the Right Home at an Affordable Price   *29*

Options in the Home Buying Market *32*
The Ins and Outs of Financing *33*
Negotiating the Best Deal When Buying or Selling Your Home *42*
Settlement Costs *43*
Refinancing Your Home *44*
Repaying Your Mortgage *44*

3 INSURING YOUR FUTURE   49

Choosing an Insurance Agent *52*
Homeowner's Insurance *52*
Umbrella Liability Insurance *59*
Automobile Insurance *60*
Life Insurance *61*
How Much Insurance Do You Need? *68*

4 INVESTMENT ALTERNATIVES   73

An Overview—Twelve Types of Investments *75*
Investments Offered by Banks and Savings Institutions *77*
Federal Government Securities *80*
Corporate Securities *86*
Mutual Funds *89*
Money Market Mutual Funds *91*
Tax-Deferred Annuities *91*

5 YOUR CORE INVESTMENTS   93

Diversity and Liquidity: A Starting Point *96*
A Close Look at Your Mortgage *97*
Planning for a Financially Secure Retirement *98*
How to Increase Your Retirement Income *102*
Individual Retirement Accounts *103*
Planning for College Education *107*
Uniform Gift to Minors Account *108*
A Contingency Account *109*
Those Awful Car Payments *110*

6 THE DEVIL AND DOW JONES   115

Investing in Securities *117*
The Stock Market—Perspective *119*

Contents

    Stock Market Analysis   *121*
    Fundamental Analysis   *123*
    Technical Analysis   *128*
    Covered Call Option-Writing Program   *129*
    Municipal Bonds   *133*

7 INVESTING IN YOUR OWN BUSINESS AND RENTAL REAL ESTATE   **131**

    Why Invest in Your Own Business?   *139*
    A Business in Your Home—The Great Tax Advantages   *140*
    Investing in Real Estate   *143*
    What It's Like When You Own Real Estate   *144*
    Realities and Fallacies of Property Management   *145*
    Purchasing Rental Property   *147*
    Leases   *149*
    Selecting and Keeping Tenants   *150*

8 ESTATE PLANNING   **155**

    Your Will   *158*
    Selecting an Executor   *159*
    Basics of Trusts   *160*
    Investment Instructions in Your Trust?   *165*
    Management of Your Trust   *166*
    Trustee or Beneficiary as Executor?   *167*
    Selecting a Lawyer   *168*

9 BUILDING YOUR KNOWLEDGE POWER   **171**

    Introduction to a Modern Library   *173*
    Government Publications—A Cornucopia of Free Information   *175*
    Books, Books, Books   *176*
    The Home Computer—A Library on Your Screen   *176*
    Developing a Basic List of Reading Materials   *177*
    Tracking the Periodicals   *180*

INDEX   **183**

Preface

If you are like most of our friends and clients, you are concerned about the future and want to achieve financial independence. But perhaps you are confused about the whole financial scene today. You wonder where to put your money and especially what the new tax reform legislation will mean to you.

Relax! We can help you get your head on straight in the topsy-turvy world of financial planning. We don't have "gimmicky" ventures for you to invest in or any other "get rich quick" schemes in mind. *What we do have is a readable, concise, step-by-step guide to help you plan your financial goals for achieving financial independence.* All you need is the discipline to follow the plan.

This book provides you with the up-to-date information you'll need to answer these and other important financial questions:

- Should you own a home? How can you select the right home in the right location and buy it at the right price? What is the best type and length of mortgage for you? Are adjustable rate mortgages (ARMs) really a bargain? What are the pitfalls of ARMs?
- Should you refinance your home if it has a high-interest-rate mortgage? What are the costs of refinancing? How much will it

save you in the long run? Would prepaying your mortgage save you more than refinancing?
- How much homeowner's insurance should you carry on your home and its contents? How can you be sure you will recover all of your losses if you have a major fire or burglary? How much can you save on homeowner's and automobile insurance with deductibles and discounts?
- How much life insurance do you and your spouse really need? Are you paying too much for your present life insurance? Which type of life insurance is best for you: term, whole life, universal or variable?
- How can you maximize the amount of interest you collect on all your savings and minimize the amount of interest you pay?
- How can you take full advantage of all your employer's fringe benefits, especially those relating to your retirement, health and education, stock purchase, and life insurance?
- How can you set up an investment program that will pay for your children's college educations, get rid of those awful car payments, provide for the "extras" you really want, and assure a financially secure retirement?
- How should you invest your money? Are common stocks best for you? If so, how do you choose which to buy and when to sell them? Is it better to purchase shares in a mutual fund or buy individual stocks? Do savings institutions offer investment alternatives that meet your needs? Are savings bonds or other government securities right for you? What about money-market funds, municipal bonds, and tax-deferred annuities?
- How does the new tax legislation affect your individual retirement account (IRA)? Where should you invest your IRA contributions? How much will you accumulate for your retirement?
- Should you consider investing in yourself by going into business to capitalize on your interests and hobbies? Can you enjoy tax savings by operating a business from your home? Should you consider buying rental properties? What are the joys and pitfalls of property management?
- Why do you need a will? How do you select a lawyer and executor? Can a trust save both you and your beneficiaries grief *and* money?

Preface

- How can you get more financial information without paying for it?

Now join us in taking the steps toward building financial independence.

Robert E. Pritchard
Gregory C. Potter
Larry E. Howe

Glassboro, New Jersey

Acknowledgments

Many of the ideas presented in *Be Your Own Financial Advisor* were suggested by professional colleagues and business principals who reviewed individual chapters of the book. We would like especially to acknowledge the help provided by the following people: **Leo C. Beebe,** chairman and CEO, K-Tron International, Inc., Pitman, N.J.; **Nate Berman,** life insurance specialist, Stockwell-Harmer Insurance Co., Collingswood, N.J.; **James J. Devlin,** insurance officer, Presbyterian Ministers Fund, Philadelphia; **James W. DuBois,** CLU, financial planner, Turnersville, N.J.; **Roy E. Duffield,** G.R.I., real estate broker, Wenonah, N.J.; **Thomas L. Earp,** Esq., Archer and Greiner, a professional association, Haddonfield, N.J.; **John Gartmann,** professional real estate manager and president, Gartmann Associates, Inc., Delran, N.J.; **Mary Ann S. Humbert,** manager, Hillcrest Home and Land Co., Pitman, N.J.

Also: **Allana L. Liverman,** vice-president, First Fidelity Bank, N.A., South Jersey, Burlington; **Thomas P. Mahoney,** loan officer, Marlton, N.J.; **Michael J. Minyon,** insurance specialist, Stockwell-Harmer Insurance Co., Collingswood, N.J.; **Donald H. Savage,** Field Corporate Relations Manager, Allstate, Basking Ridge, N.J.; **C. Fred Stinner,** insurance specialist, T.M. Meadows, Inc., Pitman, N.J.;

William P. Wallace, president, Preferred Marketing Associates and real estate investor, Wenonah, N.J.

We would also like to acknowledge the assistance and useful comments of those colleagues who reviewed the manuscript in its entirety: **John C. Benstead,** CPA, tax partner, Deloitte, Haskins and Sells, Cherry Hill, N.J.; **James L. Capobianco,** MBA, Esq., practicing tax and estate specialist, Sewell, N.J.; **Louise Capobianco,** assistant vice president, First Fidelity Bank, Philadelphia; **Vincent Casella,** member, Philadelphia Stock Exchange; **Thomas J. Hindelang,** DBA, CPA, Chairperson, Dept. of Finance, Drexel University, Philadelphia; **Millard I. Jackson, Jr., Esq.,** vice president of Financial Planning, Janney Montgomery Scott, Philadelphia

Also: **Robert R. Kugler,** Esq., chairman, Real Estate Department, Archer and Greiner, a professional corporation, Haddonfield, N.J.; **Warren R. Pierce, Jr.,** executive vice president, First Fidelity Bank, N.A., South Jersey, Woodbury; **William F. Powell,** vice president, Janney Montgomery Scott, Woodbury, N.J.; **John V. Riso,** vice president and senior trust officer, First Fidelity Bank, N.A., South Jersey, Woodbury; **Sandor Szilassy,** LL.D., director of Library Services, Glassboro State College, N.J.; **Margaret M. Van Brunt,** CPA, tax specialist and professor of Taxation, Glassboro State College, N.J.; **Lisa C. Woodman,** MBA, CPA, staff accountant, International Trade Administration

We also would like to express our sincere thanks to Jeffrey A. Krames, business editor at Prentice Hall, for his efforts in getting this book published in a timely manner to meet your needs.

Finally, we express our most sincere appreciation to Linda B. Johnson for her expert preparation of this manuscript for publication.

Join us now and become *your own* financial advisor.

1

KEEPING THE HORSE AHEAD OF THE CART

"If you think nobody cares if you're alive, try missing a couple of car payments."

earl wilson

If you are like most of our friends and clients, you are concerned about the future and want to achieve financial independence. You also want to become independent of the many financial advisors who want to sell you products or services you may not need, but you may be uncertain about the financial outlook today. The economic picture indeed is changing very rapidly. Who, for example, would have thought in 1980 that "affluent" Houston, Texas, would be in a recession in 1987? Would you have guessed that the real cost of gasoline (after inflation) would be less now than before the Arab oil embargo of the '70s? Could you have imagined four years ago that automobiles would be imported from South Korea and Yugoslavia? And who would have guessed that the Midwest would be in a recession while states along the East and West Coasts would be enjoying growth economies?

Yes, change is all around us. You wonder what this means to your own pocketbook—what should you do to get ahead and stay ahead financially in these changing times? In the following chapters we will prepare you to assume the role of your own financial advisor. We don't have any "gimmicky" investment ventures or other "get-rich-quick" schemes. *What we do have is a readable, concise, step-by-step guide to help you plan your financial goals for achieving financial independence.* All you need is the discipline to follow the plan. Here are some of the important questions relating to that plan:

- How can you establish realistic financial goals? What are the best ways to save and invest for you and your family?
- Should you own a home? How can you select the right home at the right location and buy it at the right price? What is the best type and length of mortgage for you? Are adjustable rate mortgages (ARMs) really a bargain? What are the pitfalls of ARMs?
- Should you refinance your home if it has a high-interest mortgage? What are the costs of refinancing? How much will it save you in the long run? Would prepaying your mortgage save you more than refinancing?

- How much homeowner's insurance should you carry on your home and its contents? How can you be sure that you will recover all of your losses if you have a major fire or burglary? How much can deductibles and discounts save you on homeowner's and automobile insurance?
- How much life insurance do you and your spouse really need? Are you paying too much for your present life insurance? Which type of life insurance is best for you—term, whole life, universal, or variable?
- How can you maximize the amount of interest you collect on all your savings and minimize the amount of interest you pay?
- How can you take full advantage of all your employer fringe benefits, especially those relating to your retirement, health and education, stock purchase, and life insurance?
- How can you set up an investment program that will pay for your children's college educations, get rid of those awful car payments, provide for the "extras" you really want, and assure a financially secure retirement?
- How should you invest your money? Are common stocks best for you? If so, how do you choose which ones to buy and when to sell them? Is it better to purchase shares in a mutual fund or purchase individual stocks? Do savings institutions offer investment alternatives that meet your needs? Are savings bonds or other government securities right for you? What about money-market funds, municipal bonds, and tax-deferred annuities?
- How does the Tax Reform Act of 1986 affect your individual retirement account (IRA)? Where should you invest your IRA contributions? How much will you accumulate for your retirement?
- Should you consider investing in yourself by going into business to capitalize on your interests and hobbies? Can you enjoy tax savings by operating a business from your home? Should you consider buying rental properties? What are the joys and pitfalls of property management?
- Why do you need a will? How should you select a lawyer and executor? Can a trust save you and your beneficiaries both grief and money?
- When you want more financial information, how can you get it without paying for it?

Your financial success depends upon your building a solid foundation and developing an orderly plan to achieve your financial goals. Let's begin by looking at some of these important financial matters:

- Eliminating costly interest payments
- Starting an investment program that will lead to financial security
- Developing a savings and spending plan to help you meet your financial goals
- Taking full advantage of employer fringe benefits
- Obtaining the highest rate of interest on all your savings, including your checking account
- Establishing a "rainy day account"

MANAGING YOUR MONEY AND EMPLOYEE FRINGE BENEFITS

"Well, thank goodness they're giving up on this bill—it says it's their final notice."

Managing your money is a key element in attaining financial independence. One financial advisor we know comments that the difference between a rich person and a poor person is that the rich person collects interest while the poor person pays it. Although this is not always true, it provides a good starting philosophy for financial management. We recommend that you consider the following recommendations to start you toward financial independence:

1. *Avoid monthly service charges on your checking account* by maintaining a "minimum required balance" in your checking account. Service charges on checking accounts can be very expensive. Try to avoid them.

2. *Change your checking account to a "NOW Account"* (a Negotiable Order of Withdrawal Account). A NOW Account is very similar to an ordinary checking account except that *it pays interest* and requires a minimum balance in your account at all times (usually $500 to $1,000). If you don't have sufficient funds to maintain the minimum balance right now, plan to regularly increase your checking account balance so that you will be able to have a NOW account and collect interest.

Although the rate of interest on a NOW Account won't be very high, you likely will receive more interest than you expect. The reason is simple. Your account almost always has more money in it than your checkbook balance shows. Until a check which you have written is deposited and clears your bank, you receive interest on the money in your account. Let's suppose you pay the electric bill on the eighth day of the month. The check may not clear for five days to two weeks—perhaps not until the 15th of the month. You receive interest for an extra week on the amount withdrawn. Over the period of a year, that interest will add up.

3. *Arrange for your pay to be deposited directly into your checking account or NOW Account.* If possible, use electronic funds transfer. It's fast and efficient and does not depend on the mail. It also assures that you will receive maximum interest on your money if you have a NOW Account.

4. *If possible, consider having mortgage and other monthly payments made automatically by your bank the day they are due.* If you own a home, your mortgage payment is most important, since it obviously represents a large amount of money, and you certainly don't want to be late. But there's no reason to pay it before it's actually due. Automatic transfer assures that the payments will be made on the day they are due.

Before you initiate automatic payments, review the statements from your checking or NOW Account for the past few months. Note when large checks cleared your account and compare this date with the date you wrote the check. The period of time between the date you wrote the check and the date the bank pays it and debits your account is called the "float." Suppose, for example, your mortgage is due on the first of the month, and you typically mail your payment by the 28th of the month to make sure you're on time. The check arrives at the mortgage company on the first, and your account is credited with the payment.

If the check does not normally clear your bank for ten days (the float period), then initiating an automatic payment on the first of the month would not be to your advantage. If you have a NOW Account, for example, you would lose several days interest on the amount of your check to the mortgage company.

5. *If you use credit cards, shop around to find those that charge the lowest interest rates.* Both you and your spouse should have separate accounts so that each of you will have established credit histories. When you use credit cards, *always pay the bills completely when they are due.*

If you presently have outstanding credit card charge balances, pay them off as soon as possible. Many credit card accounts charge 18 to 20 percent interest. This is the *most expensive* way to borrow. Also keep in

Managing Your Money and Employee Fringe Benefits

mind that many credit cards have a yearly fee ranging from $20 to $35 or more. So limit yourself to just one card.

6. *Establish a rainy day account.* We recommend that you consider using a money market account at your savings institution to keep your "rainy day account." (Money market accounts are discussed in Chapter 4.)

Maintain the equivalent of approximately three months of take-home salary in your "rainy day account." It may take some time for you to build up this account. Be patient; it is very important to your financial security. If your spouse works, he or she also should maintain a "rainy day account." Keep these accounts in individual names, rather than jointly. If you or your spouse should die, the survivor may face severe restrictions on withdrawals if the money is in a joint account.

Keeping funds in individual accounts does have a disadvantage. If one spouse should become sick, for example, the other may not have the access to needed funds. A simple way to solve this problem is for each spouse to give power of attorney to his or her account to the other spouse. This is not complicated; a lawyer is not needed. Generally, all that is necessary is to fill out a "power of attorney signature card" for the account. The savings institution should have such cards readily available.

Don't spend your "rainy day accounts." You may be tempted to purchase some "big ticket" item when you have accumulated some money in this account. Don't do it. Save for big purchases as described in Chapter 5.

7. *Develop a spending and saving plan.* This need not be a burdensome task, but it will force you to set financial goals. Don't begin your plan with expenditures and hope you'll wind up with "extra money" for possible investment. Decide first how much you want to put aside for investment each month. Even if you can only put away $20 or $30 each month, systematic saving can have a profound effect on your financial situation in years to come. Make saving your first priority (pay yourself first!). Payroll withholding is a good way to accomplish this goal. The savings are withheld by your employer and deposited directly into an account of your choice. Having never really received the money in your take-home pay, you'll be less likely to miss it.

8. *As your salary increases, plan to save more.* You probably receive salary increases each year, sometimes more frequently. Those extra dollars can slip through your hands almost unnoticed. Don't allow this to happen. *We recommend that you try to save one out of every four*

additional dollars of take-home pay when you receive an increase in your salary.

9. *Look closely at your employment fringe benefits.* Some companies offer valuable savings plans. For example, they may contribute 50 cents to your account for every dollar you save. Normally these plans limit your contribution to a maximum of 6 percent of your gross pay. This is such a good deal that we recommend it as a first order of investment. You may have a choice of investing your contribution as well as that of your employer in U.S. Savings Bonds, company stock, or a mutual fund. How you invest the money should be decided on the basis of information provided in following chapters. A note of caution: Frequently you must leave your contribution in the plan for a minimum of three years or your employer's contribution will be withdrawn.

Many employers offer *pension plans* which permit you to contribute a portion of your salary on a tax-deferred basis to the plan. "Tax deferred" means that you do not have to pay any *federal* income tax on those earnings which you contribute in the year the contributions are made. Whether your contribution is subject to state income tax in the contribution year varies among states. The money is, however, subject to tax when you retire and receive it as a part of your pension.

Two negatives should be discussed here. First, once the money is contributed, you may not be able to recover it until retirement, unless you are disabled. Second, you lose control of the money. Someone else (a pension fund manager, for example) manages your money. Of course, if you don't want to manage the money, or feel you are not competent to do so, then this may be an advantage. We recommend that you postpone any decisions pertaining to adding to your pension until you have read the following chapters.

Finally, take the time to consult with your employer's personnel representative so that you completely understand all of the financial fringe benefits available to you.

10. *Examine your health, disability, and life insurance benefits with your employer's personnel representative.* Determine the coverages provided and the cost of any optional coverages, such as dental and eye glasses. Review both the history of your costs in these areas and any anticipated costs; for example, will your children need braces? Then determine which, if any, optional coverages you need. Also review the limits on medical insurance coverage. Do you need to purchase additional insurance that provides coverage beyond the maximum limits of your employer's policy?

Managing Your Money and Employee Fringe Benefits 9

Determine your group life insurance coverage. Does it increase as your salary increases? Use this information when determining the additional coverage you need, if any, as described in Chapter 3. Finally, check your disability insurance coverage. If your employer does not provide sufficient disability insurance, consider purchasing your own policy. Discuss this with your insurance agent.

11. *Examine your educational benefits with your employer's personnel representative.* Many companies provide on-the-job training, tuition reimbursement, and seminar or certification programs. Investing your time to develop additional career skills or to obtain a license, certification, or degree is highly recommended—especially if your employer will pay for it. The financial return on such investments usually is very great and continues throughout your working life, also enhancing your retirement benefits, too.

12. *Consider an Individual Retirement Account (IRA).* Even with current limitations under the Tax Reform Act of 1986, we view IRAs as an important step in establishing long-term financial security for many people. Even if you and your spouse are both covered by pensions, IRAs should be considered as a supplement. See Chapter 5 for more information about IRAs.

13. *Carefully check interest rates before borrowing money.* Many unscrupulous lenders will mislead you by offering financing at rates which appear to be low. For example, suppose you are borrowing $8,000 to purchase a car. A lender offers you an 8 percent loan for four years (48 months), with interest and payments calculated as follows:

The interest is 8 percent of $8,000, or $640 per year for four years—a total of $2,560. This amount the unscrupulous lender adds to the $8,000 for a total of $10,560. The payments are determined by dividing the $10,560 by 48, or $220 per month.

Actually, however, you owe the entire $8,000 for only one month. When you make a payment at the end of each month, the principal (the amount you borrowed) is reduced. Thus, at the end of the first month you might only owe $7,980. But the interest calculation described above includes interest on the $8,000 for the entire four years. Consequently, the "true" interest rate on the loan we have described here, which is called the Annual Percentage Rate (APR), is actually about 15 percent, not 8 percent. *Always request the APR* when borrowing money. All lenders are required by law to disclose the Annual Percentage Rate.

14. *Avoid financing purchases whenever possible.* Buying now and paying later is simply mortgaging your future. Of course, almost every-

one needs to borrow to purchase a home. But when it comes to purchasing automobiles, appliances, or other entertainment items, avoid financing if at all possible. Save for what you need, and don't believe the argument that "you can drive out in that new car for only $260 per month for the next four years." If you saved $260 per month for four years at an 8 percent annual rate, you would have $14,650.94! If you purchase the new car, you will have a four-year-old car in four years and an empty pocketbook. *Don't get hooked on making purchases because you can afford the "low monthly payments."* See Chapter Five for a plan to avoid those "awful car payments."

15. *Check the tax deductibility of interest before you borrow.* Under the Tax Reform Act of 1986, the tax deductibility of interest on consumer loans (credit cards, automobiles, insurance policies) is being phased out over a five-year period. If you do need to borrow money, you may want to consider a *home equity loan.*

HOME EQUITY LOANS

Home equity loans (HELS) have been around for a long time, but were never marketed as aggressively as they have been in recent months. Lending institutions are spending millions advertising these loans because HELS represent a potentially very profitable market, since homeowners almost always have above average incomes and frequently sufficient income to cover additional loan payments. Furthermore, the interest on many HELS is tax deductible, as we will see. The tax deductibility of interest has heightened consumer awareness of these loans. Although the interest deductibility of most other loans (except mortgages) is being phased out under the Tax Reform Act of 1986, the tax deductibility of interest on many home equity loans has remained intact.

Many lending institutions will extend HELS up to 80 percent or more of a home's fair market value, less the amount of outstanding mortgages. Thus, if you owned a home with a fair market value of $100,000 and owed $50,000 on an existing mortgage, you probably could borrow at least another $30,000. Most HELS are approved as credit lines. Once the credit line is approved, the borrower may use it whenever he or she wishes and for virtually any purpose.

But just because you may be able to borrow $30,000 in the form of a HEL doesn't mean the interest on that loan will be tax deductible. Tax deductibility of interest on HELS is limited. Interest payments may be

Home Equity Loans

deducted on loans for as much as the purchase price of the home, plus improvements made or the fair market value, whichever is lower. Exceptions are interest on medical and educational loans. In the preceding example, you already have a $50,000 mortgage. Suppose the purchase price of your home, plus improvements, only equalled $60,000. If you borrowed $30,000, you could only deduct interest on $10,000, unless you used the money for medical or educational purposes, or for a home improvement.

If the sum borrowed had been used for home improvements (thereby increasing the purchase price of the home plus improvements from $60,000 to $90,000), then all of the interest on the new loan would be tax deductible.

Home equity loans can be very dangerous because they are so easy to obtain, and you can spend the money almost any way you want: to purchase that new Mercedes, a boat, pay off credit card loans and reduce payments. HELS, which often have long maturities, *should really* be used to finance expenditures such as home improvements, since the equity being taken from the home in the form of the loan is returned in the form of an improvement. HELS *should not* be used to finance short-term purchases such as an auto, refrigerator or holiday gifts unless you can discipline yourself to repay the loan rapidly.

Consider for example, how you might use a HEL to borrow $10,000 to purchase a new car. An auto loan is available at 13 percent and would have 48 monthly payments of $268.28. Using a HEL with a repayment period of 20 years and an interest rate of 9 percent, the monthly payments would be only $89.97. Low payments like these are very attractive and some lending institutions will try to sell you on the idea of using a HEL to finance a car. But borrowing over a 20-year period to finance a car is clearly financially unsound. The car will be in the scrap heap long before the loan is repaid.

By contrast, 20-year financing to replace a roof or add insulation or siding, could be very sensible, although again we would recommend repaying as rapidly as possible.

The loan terms of a HEL can make borrowing attractive. Consider the example of the $10,000 loan already described above. A $10,000 siding job financed over 20 years with monthly payments of only $89.97 could be very affordable and may represent a financially prudent investment as well.

If you are considering using a HEL, you need to shop around and learn more about the loan terms being offered by various lenders in your area. Frequently, HELS involve an application fee, points, an annual fee, and some have prepayment penalties. The interest rate on most HELS is variable and generally floats at about 1.75 percent above the benchmark rate (usually the prime rate or Treasury bill rate). But there is a large spread—some institutions charge as much as 4.5 percent above the benchmark rate.

Since interest rates on most HELS are variable, they could increase dramatically if the general level of interest rates goes up. Moreover, unlike variable-rate mortgages, there frequently is no cap or upper limit on interest rates. Variability of interest rates and the lack of interest rate caps make HELS a risky form of borrowing, underscoring why they should be used very prudently.

Some lenders may waive fees and offer low introductory interest rates. You should keep apprised of these savings and also of the repayment terms which may vary among lending institutions in your area.

Repayment terms on HELS are being offered in a variety of forms. Of course, regardless of the principal repayment plan, monthly payments will change if interest rates change. Some lenders require monthly payment of interest only, with repayment of principal in the form of a balloon at the end of the loan period. These loans are attractive, since they have the lowest monthly payments, but are obviously risky. Other institutions require borrowers to repay a percentage of the outstanding balance each month—frequently about 2 percent. Finally, many institutions amortize the payments in the same manner as they do for mortgages.

ESTABLISHING FINANCIAL GOALS

"Most people don't plan to fail—they fail to plan!"

Your financial house is starting to take shape. You are examining options available to you. You have a good understanding of your employer's fringe benefit package. You understand the importance of having a "rainy day account" and a NOW Account that pays you interest. You plan to eliminate charge account interest payments, and you have started to save both for investment and for your future purchases. The foundation for your continued financial health is well established. So move forward to being a financial success!

Success is only a matter of luck—ask anyone who has failed. Some people feel that only certain persons are destined to succeed. We are

Establishing Financial Goals

determined to succeed and would rather stake our futures on a base of solid planning combined with hard work than worry about destiny. Join us!

We believe that the key to success is good, realistic planning. The product of planning is a personal financial plan—a plan to take you from where you are to where you want to be in five, ten, or 20 years.

One of the authors and his wife held a meeting to discuss long-range financial plans. They planned for this meeting well in advance so that each could take the time to prepare. When they met, they asked each other, "What would you like to be doing in the coming years?" Both agreed that they wanted the *option* to retire from their regular jobs at age 55. This is not to say, of course, that they definitely would retire; rather, they would like to have the financial resources to retire *if they so choose*. Naturally, it's easier to discuss such an option than it is to map out a specific course of action to accomplish it.

The key word here is *option*. We do not want to commit ourselves to precise plans. Who knows how you will feel when you get to be 55, 65, 70, or older. You may want to work full time or part time. Your health obviously will be a big factor. But for us, the goal of long-range financial planning is to provide *options* for the future rather than to lock ourselves into a specific plan.

As a part of their planning, the author and his wife decided that they would like to accumulate substantial financial resources. That might seem like every person's goal. After all, money won't bring you happiness, but it can make misery much more pleasant. *However, in making a conscious decision to accumulate financial resources, two important and related tradeoffs had to be made.*

The first has to do with current spending versus saving. They decided, for example, to fully fund their pension plans, purchase individual retirement accounts each year, and—perhaps the most important—remain in their present, conservative home rather than buying a bigger, more expensive one. They also decided to keep their automobiles for a longer period of time.

The second tradeoff concerns their investment plans. They decided to invest a percentage of their incomes each month. They evaluated the alternatives described in subsequent chapters and agreed upon a group of investments that met their needs.

As a part of their investment program, they plan to purchase a smaller property which they might want to live in after retirement. Their goal is to rent the property and make alterations to suit themselves. Then, if they want to spend winters in a warm climate or travel, they will sell their current home and move into the smaller property.

We want to caution you that owning rental real estate may not be the best choice for you (see Chapter 7). Rather, we simply want to point out that owning rental property is but one of several options you may want to consider.

Your plan likely will be much different from the example we have just given. But there is one overriding principle in every plan: *Retain flexibility by planning for options rather than making precise plans.* The world is changing much too rapidly to make definite plans for the next ten or 20 years.

SOME BASICS ABOUT INTEREST

Understanding interest is critical to your financial planning and success. We suggest that you read this section carefully, as it will impact nearly all of your important financial decisions.

Interest can be thought of as the rent you pay when you borrow money or that you receive when you save money. When you borrow, you want to pay a low rate, and when you save, you obviously would like to get a high rate. But what is "high" or "low"? A 14 percent return might not be better than a 7 percent return!

Here's why. *The real interest rate is the difference between the rate you are paying or collecting and the inflation rate, on an after-tax basis.* For example, a few years ago, you could obtain a 14 percent return on a savings certificate (described in Chapter 4) at a local savings institution. But inflation was 12 percent. Therefore, your real return before tax was only 2 percent. On an after-tax basis—assuming a 28 percent tax rate— the return actually was negative, as shown in the following calculation.

In real dollars, your wealth actually decreased from $1,000 to $968.70!

By contrast, an 8 percent return at a time when inflation is, say, 4 percent could mean an increase in your wealth. On $1,000, you would receive $80 in interest and pay $22.40 of this amount in taxes, leaving you with a total of $1,057.60 at the end of the year. With an inflation rate of 4 percent, money at the end of the year has 96 percent of the purchasing power it had at the start of the year. Consequently, your year-end purchasing power would be $1,015.30. Your wealth clearly increased.

Investment at start of year	$1,000.00
Interest (14%)	+ 140.00
	$1,140.00
Tax on interest (28%)	− 39.20
	$1,100.80
Loss from 12% inflation	− 132.10
Purchasing power at year's end	$ 968.70

When determining the impact of interest on your saving or on your borrowing, you must consider the inflation rate and the tax implications. Inflation rates differ by region. The Northeast, for instance, might experience greater inflation than the Midwest. Also, your rate of inflation may be greater or less than the national or regional averages. If you own a home, any changes in national or regional inflation rates which are influenced by changes in property values may have little actual effect on you.

COMPOUND INTEREST—THE EIGHTH WONDER OF THE WORLD

Before we go any further into a discussion of investments, we would like to introduce you to an almost "magical" financial principle: *compound interest*. If you take time to read this section, you will have an understanding of one of the most important elements that underpins all of your financial planning.

Three important aspects of compound interest need to be considered:

1. *Compound interest takes time to make a significant difference in total accumulation.* For example, if you invest $1,000 at 8 percent for one year, the interest will be $80. If the rate of interest were 10 percent, the return would be $100, a difference of only $20. By contrast, if the

same $1,000 is invested at 8 percent and 10 percent, respectively, for 15 years, the interest would be $3,172 and $4,177, respectively, a difference of over $1,000. *It takes time for compounding to have an effect.* See Table 1-1 for some interesting comparisons.

The effects of differences in interest rates can be demonstrated with IRAs. If $2,000 is contributed at the end of each year for five years, the accumulations at 8 percent and 10 percent will be $11,733 and $12,210, respectively (a difference of only $477). But in 20 years, the accumulations will be $91,524 and $114,550—a difference of $23,026. See Table 1-2 for further comparisons.

Although the figures shown in Tables 1-1 and 1-2 clearly demonstrate the advantages of receiving higher rates of interest, you should note that those investments which, on average, yield higher returns almost always expose the investor to greater risk. Common stocks as a group yield higher returns than insured bank deposits. But you can lose money in the stock market. You should make investment decisions that you are comfortable with. This is why it's so important to understand the numerous investment options available to you before making any decisions.

A third example of the effect of time can be shown with borrowing. Suppose you need a $7,000 loan for 36 months. At 11 percent, the payments would be $229.17 per month; at 13 percent, $235.86. The difference in payments is only $6.69 per month, and the total *difference* in interest over the 36 months is only $240.84. By contrast, if you were to borrow the same $7,000 for 30 years (as might be the case with a mortgage), the payments would be, respectively, $66.66 and $77.43, a difference of only $10.77 per month, but a difference in total interest over 360 months of $3,877. To add realism to the example, suppose the mortgage were $70,000 rather than $7,000. The difference in interest over the 360 months would be $38,777! Small differences in the rates of

TABLE 1-1 Growth of $1,000 at Varying Interest Rates

Interest Rate in percent	5	10	15	20
6	$1,338	$1,791	$2,397	$3,207
8	1,469	2,159	3,172	4,661
10	1,611	2,594	4,177	6,278
12	1,762	3,106	5,474	9,646
14	1,925	3,707	7,138	13,744

Compound Interest—The Eighth Wonder of the World

TABLE 1-2 Growth of Year-End $2,000 IRA Contributions

Interest Rate in percent	Year			
	5	10	15	20
6	$11,274	$26,362	$46,552	$73,571
8	11,733	28,973	54,304	91,524
10	12,210	31,875	63,545	114,550
12	12,706	35,097	74,559	144,105
14	13,220	38,675	87,685	182,050

interest you pay on loans will result in large differences in the number of dollars you pay.

2. *The stated interest rate and the effective interest rate* (sometimes called the yield) are different if interest is compounded more than once a year. For example, the effective rate (yield) of 10 percent compounded quarterly is 10.38 percent. *When performing interest calculations, it is necessary to use the effective rate of interest,* not the stated rate. Savings institutions should provide you with the effective rate on their accounts. They are required to do so by law.

3. *The higher the interest rate, the greater the effect of small changes in interest rates on the total accumulation.* For example, as noted earlier, the difference in a 20-year IRA accumulation at 8 percent and 10 percent is $23,026. The difference, however, between the accumulation at 12 percent and 14 percent is $37,945, as shown in Table 2. The actual accumulations are $144,105 and $182,050, respectively. Thus, *when interest rates are high, small changes in the rate have a dramatic effect in total interest collected* (in the case of an investment), or the total interest paid (in the case of a loan).

If the $70,000 mortgage described earlier were financed at 15 percent for 30 years, the payments would be $885.11 per month versus $774.34 at 13 percent and $666.63 at 11 percent. If the rate were 15 percent, and the borrower had no alternative but to borrow at that rate, he or she should consider a shorter term, such as 20 or 15 years. The payments would be $921.74 for 20 years ($36.64 more) and $979.71 for 15 years ($94.60 more). The savings in interest using the 20-year repayment plan versus the 30-year plan would be $97,420. The savings using the 15-year versus the 30-year would be $142,292. Mortgages are described in greater detail in Chapters 2 and 5.

CAPITALIZING ON COMPOUND INTEREST

Based on the properties of compound interest, you should follow the guidelines listed below when saving and borrowing.

1. *Always use the effective interest rate when performing calculations.*

2. *When borrowing, always insist that you be provided with the Annual Percentage Rate (APR).*

3. *When borrowing short-term* (three years or less), try to obtain the best rate, unless you are borrowing a small amount. In that case, other factors in selecting the lender may be more important than the interest rate.

4. *When borrowing long-term at times when interest rates are high,* search for the lowest rate and plan to borrow for as short a period as possible (20 years rather than 30). Also, avoid loan agreements which incorporate stiff penalties for early repayment or renegotiation of interest rates if they should increase. Then repay the loan as rapidly as possible.

5. *When you borrow long-term at times of low interest rates,* search for the lowest rate. Avoid a loan agreement which permits the lender to renegotiate the interest rate upward if interest rates increase (such as an adjustable interest rate mortgage), unless the lender will provide a substantial reduction in the initial interest rate. If you borrow long-term with an adjustable rate loan, try to repay it quickly in order to avoid potential large increases in payments if interest rates should rise. (Adjustable-rate mortgages are discussed in Chapter 2.)

6. *When saving for a long period,* monitor interest rates closely and switch your funds among investments as necessary to obtain the highest return within prudent limits of exposure to risk.

BASICS OF INVESTMENTS—STARTING YOUR INVESTMENT PROGRAM

"Experience is knowing a lot of things you shouldn't do."
William S. Knudsen

With your goals established and a plan for saving under way, now is the time to consider the various investment alternatives described in the following chapters. Before considering these alternatives, we ask that you examine the following very important *basics of good investing:*

Basics of Investments—Starting Your Investment Program

1. *Although saving money may not always be easy, deciding what to do with your savings is the really difficult part of investing.*

2. *Investing money wisely takes time and hard work.* There is no easy way to attain financial independence, but you can become your own best financial advisor.

3. *Only invest in what you understand.* If you are knowledgeable about antiques and can shop wisely and sell profitably, you may want to concentrate your investments in them. Many people have accumulated substantial wealth through collectibles—and had fun at the same time. You may be able to turn your hobby into your financial security.

4. *Don't be fooled by "hot tips."* By the time you hear the "inside news," it's not news any more. Never make investments on casual "tips."

5. *Many people would like to make a profit by helping you invest.* Stockbrokers are paid commissions when you purchase and sell securities. Savings institutions charge borrowers about 3 percent more than they pay savers. Coin and stamp dealers profit on their sales. The more you know, the less you will need to depend on the assistance of brokers, dealers, and other intermediaries. (See Chapter Nine for information on using your library to help you become more knowledgeable and independent.) Not only can you save on fees, but you also may save yourself from a bad investment.

6. *A key to financial independence is systematic savings coupled with an investment program you understand and are comfortable with.* Don't become discouraged if your progress isn't as fast as you would like. Keep at it!

7. *Diversification is important.* Even if stock, antiques, or real estate is your primary investment, don't put all your money into just one area. A diversified portfolio will help you minimize your risk.

8. *Don't forget about inflation.* As noted earlier, inflation may vary appreciably from period to period and erode the purchasing power of your income and savings. The effects of inflation must be considered in every investment decision.

9. *The tax ramifications of major investments must be considered.* You probably will require periodic assistance from your tax advisor or accountant.

10. *Financial plans will change from time to time.* Plan to monitor your plan regularly and, with your spouse, update it periodically to assure that it will continue to meet your needs for the years ahead.

LET'S SUM UP

In this chapter, we took a close look at managing your money, especially in the use of credit. We also pointed out the need to build a "rainy day account" and to check with your employer to find out your retirement benefits and options. In addition, we looked at IRAs, home equity loans, and the tax implications of borrowing money. As a particular incentive to encourage you to save, we showed you one of the greatest financial "deals" in the world: Compound interest!

With your financial house in order and your financial goals in place, you are now ready to consider investment alternatives. Your goal of financial independence will take time and energy, but persevere! Remember the wonders of compound interest.

2

THERE'S NO PLACE LIKE HOME

A homeowner visited his banker and asked, "Are you worried about my ability to repay my mortgage?"
"Yes," confirmed the banker.
"Good," said the homeowner. "That's why I'm paying you 10 percent interest!"

For most people, home ownership is the single most important investment decision. Over time, your home probably will become your single largest investment. Its value likely will increase with inflation and act as a hedge against inflation. If necessary, your home can become the basis for borrowing. This fact has become more important since the imposition of restrictions on interest tax deductibility under the Tax Reform Act of 1986, as noted in Chapter 1. We believe that for most people, home ownership is the cornerstone of financial independence.

In this chapter we look at these important financial concerns:

- The purchase of a home, townhouse, or condo
- Refinancing a home
- Obtaining the best mortgage to meet your needs
- Accelerating your mortgage payments
- Getting the best sale price for your home
- Renting an apartment

FIVE GOOD REASONS TO OWN A HOME

Owning your own home represents the first step toward achieving your financial independence. Here are five good reasons:

1. *The price of housing, including renting, will continue to increase.* This is simply a matter of supply and demand. As the population increases and the amount of land remains constant, prices will continue to go up and up. If you buy in a *good location,* you can be quite certain that the value of your home will increase, and frequently at a *faster rate* than the general level of inflation. The characteristics of a "good location" are discussed later in this chapter.

2. *Home ownership is one of the few ways you can build substantial equity* (equity = the fair market value of your home less the amount you still owe on your mortgage and any home equity loans). A portion of your mortgage payment (the principal) represents the repayment of your debt.

As you pay off your mortgage, your equity increases. Also, as property values increase, your equity increases. By contrast, you do not develop any equity when you pay rent. You might argue that since you can't spend the equity in your home, equity really is of limited value. However, this simply is not true. It is possible to borrow against your equity using a home equity loan, for example. Also, your *home equity provides a solid base for all your other investments.*

3. *On the average, once you own your home, the cost of home ownership does not increase as rapidly as the cost of renting.* The reason is simple. Most mortgage payments remain constant over the life of the mortgage, whereas rents go up from year to year.

4. *Home owners enjoy tax breaks that are not available to renters.* Mortgage interest and property taxes, for example, are tax deductible if you itemize your Federal tax deductions. Also, if you have sufficient equity in your home, you may be able to borrow against it for major purchases. As noted in Chapter 1, interest on such home equity loans is tax deductible, whereas the interest deductibility of consumer loans is being phased out.

5. *Rents are expected to increase rapidly during the next few years.* Prior to the 1986 Tax Reform Act, there were three financial incentives for owning rental properties: Rental income, rapid depreciation tax write-offs, and favorable tax treatment of long-term capital gains resulting from property appreciation.

The second and third of these have been eliminated, leaving rental income as essentially the only incentive to own rental property in a low-inflation economy. A conservative financial analysis would suggest that fewer apartments will be built in the future and therefore rents will increase dramatically. Consequently, this is a good time for the renter to buy. By contrast, if you are considering giving up home ownership and renting an apartment, be very cautious and expect your rent to increase.

SHOULD EVERYONE OWN A HOME?

Nearly everyone can benefit from home ownership. Single people, who typically are renters, can enjoy the same benefits of home ownership as married couples. If you can't afford a home on just one salary, consider forming a partnership.

Is there anyone who shouldn't purchase a home? Those who plan to relocate in the near future probably should not invest in a home. To break even, your home must appreciate at least enough to cover the closing costs at the time of purchase and sale. Closing costs, also called settlement costs, are discussed later in this chapter.

Those who just can't handle the responsibilities the typical single or detached home involves (grass cutting, shoveling sidewalks in the winter, painting, roofing repair) may find apartment living or condominiums preferable.

Some older people living on fixed incomes may want to keep their homes but feel they cannot afford to maintain them. This may be true, but some savings institutions will provide homeowners with loans to help meet current expenses. A savings and loan association might agree to provide a "reverse mortgage," lending you, let's say, $400 a month based on the equity in your home. The loan, with interest, is repaid when the house is sold. This is one way you can spend that equity we talked about earlier and continue to live in your house.

THE BEST HOME FOR YOU

> *"People who don't know whether they are coming or going are usually in the biggest hurry to get there."*

We prefer the single-family home located in a well-established neighborhood. *Location is the key to selecting a home.* Factors which determine the quality of a location are discussed later in this chapter. The single-family home affords more privacy than a condo or a townhouse.

If you can't afford a single home, consider buying a duplex and letting a renter help pay your mortgage. Of course, being a landlord does involve management responsibilities that you may be unwilling to assume. Therefore, a duplex or other multiple-family home may not be for everyone. See Chapter 7 for more information on this topic.

Condominiums are especially popular these days, but we want to alert you to some points you should consider before buying one. What exactly is a condominium? In simplest terms, a condo is a multiple-unit dwelling wherein you own one or more of the units, along with a share of the common grounds, swimming pool, tennis courts, or any other facilities. It may be similar to a high-rise apartment house, a series of town houses, or a group of two- or three-story houses. In addition to paying property taxes, you also pay a monthly management fee to cover the expense of maintaining the common property and the condo buildings.

Condo ownership involves you in an association which is responsible for maintaining the common grounds and the condo buildings. Like any other organization, it may or may not be well run. If it is not, you could be faced with unforeseen and costly maintenance charges, with a resulting hefty increase in your condo fees.

Before purchasing a condo, you should investigate how the condo fees are being managed with respect to the funding of major repairs. Talk to owners of condos in the community you are considering and look closely at the condition of the property. Is the lawn mowed regularly? Are the flowerbeds well tended? Do the units need painting? Ask for a statement showing the annual condo fee for the past five years to determine the trends in costs. Condo management will have a direct bearing on the current and future value of your condo as well as its salability.

If you're just starting out and have limited funds, do consider a town house or a condo rather than waiting until you can afford your dream home. Also, if you are an older person, you want to travel, or you have a physical handicap, consider a condo.

How About a New Development Home?

Typically everything looks new and attractive. Often special financing deals are offered to sweeten the sale, and the price may be less than a single home in an established neighborhood. New development homes are less expensive than custom-built homes but are generally more expensive per square foot than older resale homes.

Consider the following when you look at new development homes:

1. *Older development homes may not bring as high a price as a similar home in a nondevelopment neighborhood.* Many people will pay a premium to live in a neighborhood where all the homes are not similar.

2. *Those "special" financing deals offered on new development homes, condos, and town houses actually may cost you money.* Nothing is free. If a builder offers "low interest financing," you can be sure that the "savings" to you are actually included in the purchase price. Also, it's possible that the builder can't unload the houses and is simply using "lower financing" as a way of marking down the price. In this case, you really are not getting the best investment value for your dollar. Finally, if you obtain your own financing, you may be able to purchase from the builder at a lower price.

3. *When purchasing a development home,* note that introductory lower prices are frequently offered at the onset of the project, before any

houses, other than models, are constructed. Once the project is under way and families are moving into the homes, prices normally will increase.

Good buys often can be found when the project is nearing completion and only a few homes remain. The reason is simply that much of the builder's profit is made at the end of the project. The builder therefore may be anxious to close the sales office and sell the model homes.

4. *If you are purchasing a home from a builder, always check the builder's reputation.* The Better Business Bureau is a good place to start. Also, people who have already purchased homes can be asked if they have had any problems with the home or the builder. Typical homeowners in a new development, for example, will be outside working on their lawns and landscaping. If you are seriously considering purchasing a home in the development, you can drive through the area and talk with the people.

5. *When you look at the sample home in a development,* you are really looking at $15,000 worth of rental furniture and walking on the supreme, extra-cost carpet. Any imperfections on walls, flooring, and ceilings will be covered over. Moreover, space-consuming interior doors may not be present in the sample. Landscaping and a sodded lawn no doubt will add to the sample's exterior beauty, while a distracting driveway may be absent.

Ask to look at an unfinished model with the standard carpet, floor, tile, and other fixtures. The same, of course, applies to sample town houses and condos.

6. *Many development homes, condos, and town houses are built on land that looks like the Sahara Desert.* Look for mature trees or a wooded lot. If you don't find any, expect to pay higher electric bills to operate the air conditioning. Also check the "energy package" (insulation, furnace efficiency, storm windows). Newer homes generally are more energy efficient than older ones. The difference in energy efficiency may make up for the lack of shade when it comes to the monthly electric bill. But there is no substitute for mature trees to enhance the beauty and "curb appeal" of a property.

7. *Owners of new condos, town houses, and development homes may find them hard to resell.* Why should someone want to buy yours if newer ones are available? Unlike the dazzling new model down the road, your condo may have worn carpeting, soiled furniture, and faded paint. Consequently, a two- or three-year-old condo, town house, or development may be a bargain for the purchaser.

8. *Before you consider making an offer on any home,* be sure to see several houses in the same area. This "comparison shopping" is essential if you want to avoid paying too much for your home. Also, have an engineering service check all systems (electrical, plumbing, heating) to be sure everything is operating properly. Make sure that any problems identified in this survey will be fixed as part of the agreement of sale.

9. Finally, *compare the "assessed value,"* which is used for property taxes, with the asking price of those houses you are considering. Such a comparison is especially useful when shopping for houses in the same town. Although the assessed value *does not* necessarily provide a good indication of the property's fair market value, it may be used for comparison. For example, suppose House "A" is assessed at $50,000, and the price is $70,000, while House "B" is assessed at $60,000 and the price is $100,000. In this case, House "A" *may* be more realistically priced than House "B." Assessed valuation date may account for the differences in assessed values. "Equalization ratios" of assessed to market value are often published by states and may be available from the local tax assessor's office. These ratios are helpful when comparing homes located in different towns.

FINDING A GOOD LOCATION

"When it comes to purchasing real estate, there are three important factors to consider: Location, location, and location."

Finding a good location is not always easy. Let's look at some of the characteristics of a good location:

1. Good transportation to your place of work and easy access to shopping centers, schools, libraries, and other recreational and cultural facilities.

2. Homes are tidy and well-kept. Lawns are cut and shrubbery trimmed. Review zoning of vacant land to assess what your surroundings will be in the future. Also check prior use of land to assure that it wasn't used for dumping. The municipality can provide you with this information.

3. Good schools. This admittedly can be somewhat difficult to determine, but one approach might be to look at regional norms for average college aptitude test scores, as well as the percentage of students who go to college, and see how the schools in your prospective neighborhood compare.

4. New homes being built in the area are *more expensive* and more attractive than existing homes.
 5. Streets are lined with mature trees; lots are wooded.
 6. Streets are clean, lighted, and well maintained.
 7. There are no cars, boats, or trailers sitting on blocks next to homes.
 8. The neighborhood crime rate is low.

BUYING THE RIGHT HOME AT AN AFFORDABLE PRICE

The price of the home which you can afford depends primarily on the amount of *monthly mortgage payment* you are able to pay and the amount of money you have for a down payment. The monthly payment depends on three factors:

1. The amount of the mortgage
2. The interest rate
3. The length of the mortgage

To assist you in determining the size of the mortgage payment you can handle comfortably, we suggest you make up a budget to include the following items:

- Property taxes
- Water and sewer rates
- Utility costs
- Homeowner's insurance
- Mortgage creditor life insurance (life insurance for you and your spouse sufficient to pay off the mortgage if one of you should die). Life insurance is discussed in Chapter 3.

The seller should be able to provide you with copies of the property tax, water, sewer, and utility bills. The realtor can provide estimates of homeowner's and mortgage creditor life insurance costs.

To provide you with an estimate of the amount you may be qualified to borrow, we provide two basic calculations for determining your monthly payment. Although the exact percentages may change from time to time, they represent good starting points. Work through both, and then use the *lower* amount as your maximum monthly payment.

1. A buyer can afford to use 28 percent of his, her, or their monthly *gross income* for payment of mortgage interest and principal, property taxes, homeowner's insurance, condo fees, and private mortgage insurance (discussed later in this chapter). Gross income is your income before deductions.

2. A buyer can afford to use 36 percent of his, her, or their monthly *gross income* for payment of the costs in Paragraph One above, plus other *fixed monthly expenses*. Fixed monthly expenses include expenses such as car payments, alimony, child support payments, credit card revolving charge payments, and the like. Normally, the charge payment is calculated at 5 percent of your total unpaid revolving credit card balance. Fixed monthly payments would *not* include such costs as utilities, telephone, and life insurance.

Note that the rules we have outlined may vary as interest rates change. Also, higher percentages of gross income may be used in some instances for government-insured loans. A realtor may be able to "prequalify" you for a mortgage so that you will know in advance how much you may borrow.

To determine if you can afford a particular home, use the rules outlined above in conjunction with Table 2-1, as demonstrated in the following example:

You are considering a home costing $70,000. The property taxes are $1,200 per year, and the homeowner's insurance is $300. Condo fees and private mortgage costs are not applicable in this example. You will be able to make a $10,000 down payment and pay for closing costs. Thus, you need a $60,000 mortgage. Currently, mortgage rates are 10 percent. Your gross earnings are $35,000 per year. Will you qualify for a mortgage?

Step 1. 28 percent of $35,000 = $9,800. This is the total you can pay for mortgage, principal and interest, property taxes, homeowner's insurance, condo fees, and private mortgage insurance.

Step 2. Subtract property taxes and homeowner's insurance from the $9,800. $9,800 − $1,200 − $300 = $8,300. The $8,300 is the amount you can pay for mortgage, principal and interest.

Step 3. Refer to Table 2-1, the 10 percent row, 30-year column. Note the $8.78 payment per $1,000 of mortgage.

Buying the Right Home at an Affordable Price

TABLE 2-1 Equal Monthly Payments to Amortize a Loan of $1,000

Interest Rate in Percent	Length of Mortgage in Years			
	15	20	25	30
7.50	$9.27	$8.06	$7.39	$6.99
7.75	9.41	8.21	7.55	7.16
8.00	9.55	8.36	7.72	7.34
8.25	9.70	8.52	7.88	7.51
8.50	9.85	8.68	8.05	7.69
8.75	10.00	8.84	8.23	7.87
9.00	10.15	9.00	8.40	8.05
9.25	10.30	9.16	8.57	8.23
9.50	10.45	9.33	8.74	8.41
9.75	10.60	9.49	8.92	8.60
10.00	10.75	9.66	9.09	8.78
10.25	10.90	9.82	9.27	8.97
10.50	11.06	9.99	9.45	9.15
10.75	11.21	10.16	9.63	9.34
11.00	11.37	10.33	9.81	9.53
11.25	11.53	10.50	9.99	9.72
11.50	11.69	10.67	10.17	9.91
11.75	11.85	10.84	10.35	10.10
12.00	12.01	11.02	10.54	10.29
12.25	12.17	11.19	10.72	10.48
12.50	12.33	11.37	10.91	10.68
12.75	12.49	11.54	11.10	10.87
13.00	12.66	11.72	11.28	11.07
13.25	12.82	11.90	11.47	11.26
13.50	12.99	12.08	11.66	11.46
13.75	13.15	12.26	11.85	11.66
14.00	13.32	12.44	12.04	11.85
14.25	13.49	12.62	12.23	12.05
14.50	13.66	12.80	12.43	12.25
14.75	13.83	12.99	12.62	12.45
15.00	14.00	13.17	12.81	12.65
15.25	14.17	13.36	13.01	12.85
15.50	14.34	13.54	13.20	13.05
15.75	14.52	13.73	13.40	13.25
16.00	14.69	13.92	13.59	13.45

Step 4. Multiply the $8.78 by 60. (Sixty is used since you need a $60,000 mortgage.) $8.78 × 60 = $526.80. The $526.80 is the monthly payment for a $60,000, 10 percent, 30-year mortgage.

Step 5. Multiply the $526.80 monthly payment by 12 to obtain the yearly payment. 12 × $526.80 = $6,321.60.

Step 6. Compare the yearly payment (Step 5) with the amount you are able to pay (Step 2). Since you are able to pay $8,300, and the payment is $6,321.60, you should qualify for the $60,000, 10 percent, 30-year mortgage. You might want to perform similar calculations to determine if you are eligible for a shorter-length mortgage—perhaps 15 or 20 years. If you have fixed monthly expenses such as car payments, alimony, child support, or revolving credit card accounts, be sure to recalculate your eligibility using the second method described earlier.

OPTIONS IN THE HOME BUYING MARKET

With these facts in mind, here are some guidelines for selecting the right home for you:

1. *Look at homes in acceptable neighborhoods which may need only cosmetic work* (painting, yard improvement). Look carefully at the quality of construction. If you don't know much about construction, find someone who can give you an opinion. If you are concerned about the condition of wiring or plumbing, request that the homeowner give you a written mechanical or electrical system certification, or obtain an engineering survey as suggested earlier. The requirement for this certification should be included in the agreement of sale. Also include a clause which will release you from the agreement if the systems do not pass local standards or are not brought up to standard by the seller.

2. *If possible, look at unfurnished homes after someone has moved out.* Furniture may conceal possible damage to walls and floors, leaving the buyer with a false picture of the true conditions of the property. Also, it's possible that you may be overwhelmed with the furnishings and decor, which is why a furnished home often brings a higher price than a vacant one. Also remember that someone is still paying a mortgage, taxes, utilities, and maintenance on a house that may have been vacant for a long time. If you can settle soon and help the owner get rid of these expenses, you may get a bargain.

3. *Look for "handyman's specials"*—homes in otherwise acceptable neighborhoods that have been neglected. Some of these may be real bargains if you can do the carpeting, wiring, and plumbing repairs. "Handyman's specials" can save you thousands of dollars and permit you to live in a neighborhood you otherwise could not afford.

4. *Look at homes which are owned by the estates* of someone who

The Ins and Outs of Financing

has died. Heirs frequently need cash and may want to cut operating costs by selling quickly.

5. *Look at homes which have been repossessed* by lending institutions or HUD. These may be real bargains but often are hard to obtain. If the home is in a good neighborhood, 30 or 40 other people may be bidding on it. Note, however, that many have been vandalized and may have been vacant for a year or more before they are placed on the market. Moreover, you may not be able to check the plumbing or wiring prior to settlement. Drains may be clogged and electrical outlets inoperable. "Repos" are probably the best bargain for people who do their own repairs.

6. *Be aware that new homes cost 15 to 20 percent more per square foot than older homes.* A home built to your own specifications could cost even more. On a square-foot basis, you get a much better deal on a resale home than on a new home. If you are considering a new home, use the replacement-home cost estimator discussed in Chapter 3 to obtain an estimate of the construction cost.

7. *Look for "extras" when purchashing a resale home, condo, or town house.* You may get such amenities as a fence, landscaping, carpeting, fireplace equipment, or shelves in the recreation room. You may have to pay extra for some items, such as special furniture. But the cost usually is far less if the "extras" described are purchased now.

8. *Once you decide on a location and the kind of home you want, look for homes with these often-overlooked features:*

- Bathrooms with windows or, at minimum, vent fans (mildew is a constant problem)
- Linen closets in convenient locations with adequate storage space
- Bedrooms with *at least* one and one-half unbroken wall space for furniture placement
- Bedrooms with cross ventilation
- Sufficient electrical outlets in convenient locations, especially in the bedrooms and kitchen

THE INS AND OUTS OF FINANCING

"There is no economy in going to bed early to save candles if the result is twins."

If you are buying through a real estate agent, ask the agent to help you find the financing that best meets your needs. Agents are usually well connected with lending institutions and know the mortgage interest rates and closing costs for various kinds of mortgages. Closing costs depend to some extent on the kind of mortgage you obtain.

Also plan to do some shopping yourself. Call some local savings and loans and mortgage brokers to determine the rates, terms, and processing time. Look in the Yellow Pages for names of mortgage companies. Check your local newspapers, especially the Sunday section, for rates and terms offered by local lenders. A discussion of the primary types of mortgages follows, but note that large mortgage brokers may offer several variations of mortgages to meet your specific needs.

Knowledge of some basic terminology is necessary before we can discuss mortgages. First, nearly all mortgages involve the payment of one or more "discount points" (commonly called "points") to the lending institution. *A discount point is 1 percent of the mortgage and constitutes prepaid interest.*

If you are purchasing a home, the amount you pay in points may be deductible for purposes of calculating your Federal income tax liability (assuming you itemize deductions). Contact your accountant for specific information. Typically, lenders charge two to seven discount points. If you borrow $50,000, four discount points would mean an extra $2,000 in settlement charges. In addition, some mortgages involve "origination fees" (or "processing fees") and "funding fees." These fees are usually 1% of the mortgage, paid at settlement time. Finally, some mortgages involve a "mortgage insurance premium" (MIP) or "private mortgage insurance" (PMI). All of these are discussed in the following paragraphs.

Probably the most frequently used mortgage is the *conventional mortgage*. To qualify for this mortgage you need a down payment of at least 5 percent of the purchase price. (This minimum may vary from period to period.) If you have the minimum 5 percent, but less than 20 percent to put down, a private mortgage insurance charge is normally added at settlement. Note that the 5 to 20 percent range may vary by lender. The actual interest rate you pay will depend on two primary factors:

1. *The amount of your down payment.* If you can put more than 20 percent down, you may be able to negotiate a lower rate with a local savings and loan. This probably won't be possible with a mortgage company, however.

2. *The length of the mortgage.* If you can pay off the mortgage in

The Ins and Outs of Financing

15 to 20 years, you may obtain a lower rate than for a 30-year mortgage.

Lenders normally charge between two and four discount points at settlement in addition to the other settlement costs (these will be discussed in a following section). The discount points may be paid by either buyer or seller. Often if you pay the points, you can obtain the home for a lower price. This is something you must negotiate. Bear in mind that mortgage companies normally charge a 1 percent origination fee or processing fee.

The actual number of discount points typically varies with the interest rate you agree to pay and may vary by lender. For example, if you agree on a 9.5 percent rate, then you might be charged five discount points. If you pay 10 percent, three discount points might be charged. If you pay 10.5 percent, one and one-half discount points might be charged. Of course, all of the rates change from time to time. If you plan to live in the home for several years to come, it is to your advantage to take the lower rate and pay more discount points.

A second common type of mortgage is the *Federal Housing Administration–insured mortgage,* or simply FHA. FHA-insured mortgages require minimal down payment and provide up to 97 percent financing. Note that the percentage varies by region and price of home. A 1 percent origination fee normally is required, in addition to approximately a 3.8 percent mortgage insurance premium (MIP) and discount points. Keep in mind that the mortgage insurance premium changes from time to time. Moreover, the number of discount points varies with the interest rate paid—a situation similar to that of the conventional mortgage.

If you need a $50,000 mortgage, the finance charges for an FHA mortgage typically would be:

Origination fee (1%)	$500
Mortgage Insurance Premium (3.8%), which may be financed	1,900
Discount Points (three, at 1% rate). If the MIP is financed, the discount points would be based on $51,900 and would be $1,557.	1,500
TOTAL	$3,900

These charges are in addition to other settlement costs discussed in a later section. It should be noted that either buyer or seller may pay the points, or their cost may be split between them. Sometimes you can obtain a lower price if you are willing to pay the points. Again, this needs to be negotiated.

A third kind of mortgage is the *Veterans Administration guaranteed loan,* called the *VA mortgage.* You must be a veteran to be eligible. The interest rates are not negotiable and the *seller* must pay the discount points, which vary from time to time. The seller also may pay other settlement costs to enable the buyer to borrow with no down payment. A 1 percent origination fee and a 1 percent funding fee are also charged. These may be paid at the time of settlement.

If a buyer needs a $50,000 mortgage, the finance charges for a VA mortgage typically would be:

Origination Fee (1%)	$500
Funding Fee (1%)	500
Discount Points (seller must pay but they are frequently concealed in the selling price)	
TOTAL	$1,000

In many cases, existing VA mortgages may be assumed by new buyers. Thus, if you have a large amount available for a down payment, you may be able to assume the existing mortgage. Many older VA mortgages have interest rates below current mortgage rates.

Fourth, sometimes sellers will *"take back" a mortgage.* In other words, instead of borrowing from a lending institution, you borrow from the seller. Since the rate is negotiable, you may be able to borrow at a rate which is less than that offered by lending institutions or a mortgage company. As a bonus, sellers usually don't charge points, origination fees, mortgage insurance premiums, or funding fees. But most sellers who "take back" mortgages will require a substantial down payment.

Finally, you may want to consider *borrowing from a family member.* Some older people, for example, have money available and would like to obtain a return which is higher than that available from local savings institutions without exposing themselves to a great deal of risk. Lending institutions and mortgage companies typically charge about 3

The Ins and Outs of Financing

percent higher interest rates on mortgages than they pay on deposits or money they borrow. Consequently, if you borrow from a family member, you both may benefit. To explain, suppose a lending institution pays 7.5 percent on deposits and charges 10.5 percent for mortgages. If you borrowed from a relative at 9 percent, you would save 1.5 percent (plus points, origination fees, and so forth), while the lender received an extra 1.5 percent on his or her savings.

Prior to entering into a mortgage with a family member or other individual, check the interest rate with your accountant or real estate lawyer to assure that the rate is within the Internal Revenue Service's limits. There are serious tax considerations involved with loans among family members. An attorney familiar with tax law should be consulted *before* entering into such a loan. The lender should be financially secure and should not lend money which he or she may need to meet living expenses. Moreover, loans between family members should always be documented.

Within the scope of the various types of mortgages we have described, you may be able to obtain a mortgage which incorporates special payment plans to meet your needs. For example, if you have a relatively low income now but expect it to increase appreciably during the next few years, you may be able to obtain a "graduated payment mortgage." However, unless you are sure that you will be able to meet the increased payments in the future, we recommend avoiding the graduated payment mortgage.

Whatever kind of mortgage you obtain, *be sure that prepayment of principal is permitted.* Many states prohibit lending institutions from charging prepayment penalties. Prepayment of principal could save you thousands of dollars of interest payments. Prepayment of principal is discussed in a later section of this chapter and as a part of your core investments in Chapter 5.

The Mortgage Period

"Time, obviously, is relative. Two weeks on vacation is not the same as two weeks on a diet."

In many instances lending institutions will offer lower interest rates on 15- or 20-year mortgages than on 30-year mortgages. (Normally, 30 years is the longest term for a mortgage, and 10 or 15 years is the shortest.) For example, a bank or a savings and loan might charge 10.75 percent on a 30-year, fixed-rate mortgage but charge only 10.25 on a 15-

year, fixed-rate mortgage. *You may save thousands of dollars by selecting a shorter-term mortgage, especially if the interest rate is less than the longer-term alternative.*

Let's work out some figures to show the savings. Suppose you borrow $50,000 on a 10.75 percent, 30-year mortgage. The monthly payment would be $466.74 for a total of $168,026.40 over the life of the mortgage. Now let's compare a 10.25 percent, 15-year mortgage. The monthly payment would be $544.98 for a total of $98,096.40. Although the payment on the 15-year mortgage is greater by $78.24 a month, you save $69,930 in interest over the life of the mortgage. See Table 2-2 below.

Adjustable Rate Mortgages

An alternative to the fixed-rate mortgage is the adjustable-rate mortgage. An adjustable-rate mortgage usually has an initial rate about 1.5 percent lower than a fixed-rate, 15-year mortgage. If, for example, the 15-year, fixed-rate mortgage is offered at 10.25 percent, the adjustable-rate mortgage might be offered at 8.75 percent.

This may sound like a bargain, and indeed it can be. But risks are involved. As the name implies, the interest rate on an adjustable-rate mortgage can vary from year to year. Frequently the interest rate of an adjustable-rate mortgage is tied to the rate of interest paid by the U.S. government on their Treasury Bills (T-Bills). Usually, *the maximum change in the interest rate on an adjustable-rate mortgage is limited to 2 percent a year.* If the T-Bill rate were to increase by 4 percent in one year, the mortgage interest rate would increase by 2 percent.

Normally, the *maximum change in the interest rate is limited to 5 percent over the life of the mortgage.* Taking the example of an 8.75 percent, 30-year variable-rate mortgage, this means that if interest rates on T-Bills increase by 5 percent or *more,* the mortgage rate would increase from 8.75 percent to a *maximum* of 13.75 percent.

The actual annual change in the interest rate depends on the profit

TABLE 2-2 Savings Resulting From Shorter Term Mortgage

Amount Borrowed	Years	Interest Rate %	Monthly Payment	Total Payments
$50,000	30	10.75	$466.74	$168,026.40
50,000	15	10.25	544.98	98,096.40
			SAVINGS	$ 69,930.00

The Ins and Outs of Financing

the mortgage company or their lender is seeking to obtain on the loan. The profit frequently is referred to as the "margin." Suppose, for example, the lender required a 2.5 percent profit or margin above the T-Bill rate and that the T-Bill rate is 7.5 percent. Then the lender would require a minimum 10 percent rate on the mortgage. Suppose further that you borrowed using the adjustable-rate mortgage and the rate on your mortgage for the first year is 8.5 percent, plus three discount points. Recall that discount points are prepaid interest, so the lender actually is receiving 8.5 percent plus three discount points, or 11.5 percent the *first year*.

If, at the end of the first year, the T-Bill rate remains at 7½ percent, you might assume that the rate on your mortgage would remain at 8½ percent. Would it? Probably not. Since the lender wants to obtain the 2½ percent margin over the T-Bill rate, your mortgage rate likely would be raised to 10 percent.

If the T-Bill rate increased to 8.5 percent, the lender would need to raise your rate to 11 percent to obtain the 2.5 percent margin. Remember, we said that the maximum change in the interest rate on your mortgage usually is limited to 2 percent a year. Consequently, the lender could charge you only 10.5 percent for the second year, not 11 percent.

If the T-Bill rate decreased to 6.5 percent, the lender would need a 9 percent rate to obtain the 2.5 percent margin. Therefore, even if the T-Bill rate fell by 1 percent, the interest rate on your mortgage actually might increase from 8.5 percent to 9 percent.

Adjustable-rate mortgages are complex. Before obtaining such a mortgage, be sure to have a lawyer who specializes in real estate study the fine print and explain how your payments may change. Also send for a copy of "Consumer Handbook on Adjustable Rate Mortgages," published by the Federal Reserve Board and the Federal Home Loan Bank Board, 20th and Constitution NW, Washington, DC 20551.

Clearly, adjustable-rate mortgages represent a gamble. You are likely to come out ahead if:

- Interest rates decrease significantly
- You plan to own the home for a relatively short time (three years)
- Property values increase rapidly so that you can sell your home at a profit in the event your mortgage payments should become unbearable
- Your income increases to the point where you still can afford the mortgage payments on that "dream house" even if interest rates were to rise and force up your mortgage payments

Getting a Lower Interest Mortgage

Here is some basic information you need to know to help you get the best deal on your loan when purchasing or refinancing your home.

1. *Banks and particularly savings and loan associations are in the business of lending mortgage money.* They want to make a profit, and this means they look around for the best return possible. Loans to other banks or the government are very safe but don't yield high interest rates. Consequently, many financial institutions would rather lend to you. You are willing to pay a higher interest rate, but obviously you may pose a greater risk. *Your job, therefore, is to convince the lending institution that you are, in fact, a good risk.*

2. *Lenders are generally conservative.* Consequently, lenders tend to be quite cautious in evaluating loan applications. People who live at one location for a period of two or more years and have steady jobs obviously are better candidates for a loan than those who move frequently and have spotty employment records.

3. *Experienced lenders make loans based on the borrower's ability to pay interest and repay the principal in a timely manner.* Your ability to do this is directly linked to your cash flow (the amount of money left over after you have paid your taxes and met your other fixed expenses). You must be able to convince the loan officer that your cash flow will be sufficient to make the payments. You will need to provide income verification from your employer. You also will be asked to provide your income tax returns for the last two years. Finally, you may have to sign a statement documenting the source of your down payment. Lenders want to be sure that you have not borrowed the down payment from your parents, for example.

If you are receiving alimony or child support, these payments would be included as part of your income. They must be verified, however. Normally, the best way to verify payments is to ask the Probation Office (the usual agency that handles these payments) to send a statement showing the amount and date of each payment they receive. If your payments are made directly to you by your spouse, the lending institution may require another form of verification.

It might be wise to consider that any *income "paid under the table"* won't help you get the loan and likely will work against you. Lenders look for employment and income stability. Most lenders lend only on what can be verified as reportable income. If you own your own business,

The Ins and Outs of Financing

lenders may view you as a higher risk than if you work for a stable employer. The higher risk results from greater variability in your earnings. Most self-employed persons do not have paid sick-leave benefits, for example. In addition, you may be asked to have an accountant verify your income, net worth, and credit worthiness. You would do well, therefore, to get a mortgage before you change employment or go into your own business. There are exceptions, however. A new, higher paying job may satisfy income requirements that you previously might not have been able to meet.

If you have substantial existing loan payments—perhaps for a new car—your ability to pay your mortgage is reduced. Naturally, you should expect to have more difficulty getting a loan if you already have some high loan payments. Try not to buy that new car or run up a large charge account balance before you buy your home. Also, don't borrow money just before purchasing a new home, especially if you plan to use the money for a down payment or to cover settlement costs.

Finally, if you are paying alimony or child support, don't attempt to hide these obligations to make it appear that you have a greater ability to pay a mortgage. The lending institution will discover support payments in your credit evaluation. Furthermore, don't fall behind on these payments. People who are late with alimony and child support payments should expect to have their mortgage applications rejected.

4. *Lenders want to see good credit ratings.* One of the authors recently obtained a copy of his rating and found two errors, which he promptly had corrected. You should review your credit report to make sure that if reflects your credit history accurately. If your report reveals some problems, be prepared to explain each situation and how you resolved the problem. If it contains errors, contact the credit bureau and have them resolved. Incidentally, in most states, your local credit bureaus *must* provide you with a copy of your credit report.

5. *Lenders want to see a good history of mortgage payments if you already have a mortgage.* Mortgage payments do not appear on credit reports. But mortgage histories are shared among lending institutions. If you were late or missed payments on an existing mortgage, a lender will view this with greater disfavor than if you fell behind on a car payment. The lender likely will assume that a poor mortgage payment record in the past will be continued in the future.

6. *Lenders want to know to whom they are lending.* Provide up-to-date detailed resumes along with your loan application.

NEGOTIATING THE BEST DEAL WHEN BUYING OR SELLING YOUR HOME

When you are planning to purchase or sell a home, your ability as a negotiator can improve your chances of obtaining the best deal. We offer the following suggestions for your consideration:

1. *Consider trying to sell the property yourself.* This requires some work, including advertising, probably having a sign made and showing the property. You can save thousands of dollars, however, by not having to pay the real estate commission. If you do decide to sell yourself, discuss the process with a lawyer who specializes in real estate before putting your property on the market. Also be sure to take adequate security precautions before letting anyone in your home. Finally, selling a home yourself may take longer than if you use an agent. If timing is a critical factor, the savings enjoyed by selling the home yourself may not be justified.

2. If you are buying or selling through an agent, *consider negotiating face-to-face with the other party.* The agent may not like this, but you may be able to negotiate a better deal if you can discuss all the details and extras that might be involved.

3. *Never become emotionally involved.* As a buyer, you cannot expect to get the best deal if you lose your objectivity by "falling in love with the house." As a seller, don't panic if your home isn't sold within two weeks. If you are forced to do something quickly, it likely will be very costly.

4. *When dealing with agents, don't let them know that you might "pay a little extra" or "take a little less."* As a buyer, make a firm offer and plan to stick to it. Remember, you can find other houses on the market. As a seller, reject "low ball" offers immediately. As an example, one of the authors put a home on the market with an agent for $125,000. Within three days, the agent had an offer for $90,000, which the seller rejected. A week later an offer for $100,000 came across. This also was rejected. Then an offer for $110,000 was made, followed by another for $118,000, and finally one for $121,000. The seller rejected all of them, took the house off the market for six months and now is attempting to sell it himself for $140,000.

5. *If you use an agent to sell your home, negotiate the commission.* Commission rates are not fixed. You may obtain just as good service at 6 percent commission as you would at 7 percent. Also, check the following:

Settlement Costs

- What marketing efforts will the agent make (for example, newspaper or journal advertising, computer networking, and so on)?
- Will the home be listed in a multiple listing service?
- Will the commission be less if the listing broker sells your home, thereby eliminating the need to split the commission with another broker?
- What happens if you find a buyer yourself?

6. *Whether you are a buyer or a seller, always use an attorney to represent you.* The attorney should review all papers before you sign them, and he or she also should represent you at settlement.

SETTLEMENT COSTS

We have already discussed those settlement costs which relate to various kinds of mortgages. There are other costs, however, and some of these have been enumerated in Table 2-3, which is in the form of a work sheet. Note, however, that this list is probably not all-inclusive.

TABLE 2-3 Settlement Charge Worksheet

Item	Your Costs
Application Fee (includes appraisal)	_____
Credit Report	_____
Discount Points	_____
Origination Fee	_____
Mortgage Insurance Premium	_____
Private Mortgage Insurance	_____
Funding Fee (VA)	_____
Survey	_____
Attorney's Fee (attorney representing lending institution)	_____
Attorney's Fee (representing you)	_____
Termite Certification	_____
Water Table Survey (some locations)	_____
Title Search and Insurance	_____
Interest Prepayment (depending on date of settlement and lending institution)	_____
Title Company Settlement Services	_____
Recording Fee	_____
Water, Sewer, and Property Taxes Paid By Seller in Advance	_____
Escrow of Property Taxes and Homeowner's Insurance	_____
Fuel Oil	_____
TOTAL	_____

Settlement can be very expensive. Therefore, it is important to shop around for the mortgage that best meets your needs. Be sure to ask your proposed lender for an itemization of all settlement fees you may be charged. You must be aware of the total costs to be sure that you have selected a home within a price range you can afford.

REFINANCING YOUR HOME

"I finally know what distinguishes man from other beasts: Financial worries."

The Journal of Jules Renard

In periods when interest rates are falling, some homeowners who purchased homes at higher rates in years past may want to know if they can lower their mortgage payments by refinancing at a lower rate. The cost to refinance your home frequently is almost as much as the cost of settlement. Since refinancing costs can vary appreciably, you should determine the exact cost from two or more prospective lenders. *Normally, if you can obtain at least a 3 percent reduction in your mortgage interest rate and you plan to own your home for two to three years, it pays to refinance.* As a rule of thumb, divide the cost to refinance by the monthly savings. The result is the number of months you must own your home to recover the financing costs.

As an aside, we should point out that most lending institutions probably would lend you the amount needed to refinance your mortgage. This loan amount could be added to the remaining principal owed on your existing mortgage.

If you want to take advantage of lower interest rates and find that the cost of refinancing is appreciable (several thousand dollars), consider prepayment of principal as an alternative to refinancing. Although prepayment will not reduce your interest rate, it will reduce the number of dollars you pay in interest over the life of your mortgage. Prepaying your mortgage is discussed in the following section.

PREPAYING YOUR MORTGAGE

By paying a little extra each month on your mortgage, you may be able to reduce the number of payments and save thousands of dollars in interest. Refer to the mortgage amortization schedule in Table 2-4 which shows

Prepaying Your Mortgage

the first 49 payments for a $50,000 mortgage at 10 percent for 30 years (360 payments). Although this is not shown on the table, it takes approximately 23½ years (283 payments) to pay half the principal. After the 283rd payment, the outstanding balance is $24,857.73. The total interest paid over 30 years is $107,954.87—which is over twice the amount borrowed.

To reduce the total length of the mortgage and the amount of interest paid, some people "double up" on principal payments. For example, if the mortgage in Table 2-4 includes an additional $22.30 (the second month's principal payment) in the first payment, this would eliminate one month from the length of the loan and save $438.79. Likewise, the *actual second payment* would include the regular principal for the third payment ($22.49). If this system is followed, the total period of the mortgage would be reduced from 30 to 15 years, and the mortgagee would save $78,982.20 in interest! Note, however, that the principal payment increases over the years, since the principal begins to assume a larger proportion of the total mortgage payment. Be sure to obtain an amortization table for your mortgage from the lender or through a lawyer so that you will be able to determine the monthly payments if you want to "double up."

Although the "doubling up" method of prepaying your mortgage is commonly used, you may instead want to add a fixed amount to each payment—perhaps $25.00 per month—and increase the amount when you get a pay raise. Whatever method you use, be sure to obtain a statement from your lender at the end of each year showing the reduction of outstanding principal you owe. Check these figures carefully to be sure that they have credited your account correctly.

Prepayment certainly could save you thousands of dollars in interest payments. It could also mean a reduction in the amount of creditor life insurance you would need. (Creditor life insurance is described in Chapter 3.) But prepayment is not always the best course of action. If, for example, your mortgage interest rate is 10 percent, and you can obtain a higher rate (perhaps 12 percent) on an insured deposit at a lending institution, you would be better advised to save at the higher rate. Likewise, if you are paying 18 percent on revolving credit charge accounts, it would be preferable to pay these loans rather than to prepay a lower rate mortgage. By contrast, if your mortgage interest rate is 10 percent, and lending institutions are paying only 7 percent interest on deposits, you would do better to add *discretionary funds* to your mortgage payment.

Remember, whenever you prepay any loan, you are spending extra

TABLE 2-4 $50,000, 10 Percent, 30-Year Mortgage Amortization Schedule

Month	Previous Balance	Interest	Payment	Reduction in Balance	New Balance
1	50000.00	416.67	438.79	22.12	49977.88
2	49977.88	416.48	438.79	22.30	49955.58
3	49955.58	416.30	438.79	22.49	49933.09
4	49933.09	416.11	438.79	22.68	49910.41
5	49910.41	415.92	438.79	22.87	49887.54
6	49887.54	415.73	438.79	23.06	49864.49
7	49864.49	415.54	438.79	23.25	49841.24
8	49841.24	415.34	438.79	23.44	49817.79
9	49817.79	415.15	438.79	23.64	49794.15
10	49794.15	414.95	438.79	23.83	49770.32
11	49770.32	414.75	438.79	24.03	49746.28
12	49746.28	414.55	438.79	24.23	49722.05
13	49722.05	414.35	438.79	24.44	49697.61
14	49697.61	414.15	438.79	24.64	49672.97
15	49672.97	413.94	438.79	24.84	49648.12
16	49648.12	413.73	438.79	25.05	49623.07
17	49623.07	413.53	438.79	25.26	49597.81
18	49597.81	413.32	438.79	25.47	49572.34
19	49572.34	413.10	438.79	25.68	49546.65
20	49546.65	412.89	438.79	25.90	49520.76
21	49520.76	412.67	438.79	26.11	49494.64
22	49494.64	412.46	438.79	26.33	49468.31
23	49468.31	412.24	438.79	26.55	49441.76
24	49441.76	412.01	438.79	26.77	49414.99
25	49414.99	411.79	438.79	26.99	49387.99
26	49387.99	411.57	438.79	27.22	49360.77
27	49360.77	411.34	438.79	27.45	49333.32
28	49333.32	411.11	438.79	27.68	49305.65
29	49305.65	410.88	438.79	27.91	49277.74
30	49277.74	410.65	438.79	28.14	49249.60
31	49249.60	410.41	438.79	28.37	49221.23
32	49221.23	410.18	438.79	28.61	49192.62
33	49192.62	409.94	438.79	28.85	49163.77
34	49163.77	409.70	438.79	29.09	49134.68
35	49134.68	409.46	438.79	29.33	49105.35
36	49105.35	409.21	438.79	29.57	49075.78
37	49075.78	408.96	438.79	29.82	49045.96
38	49045.96	408.72	438.79	30.07	49015.89
39	49015.89	408.47	438.79	30.32	48985.57
40	48985.57	408.21	438.79	30.57	48954.99
41	48954.99	407.96	438.79	30.83	48924.16
42	48924.16	407.70	438.79	31.08	48893.08
43	48893.08	407.44	438.79	31.34	48861.73
44	48861.73	407.18	438.79	31.60	48830.13
45	48830.13	406.92	438.79	31.87	48798.26
46	48798.26	406.65	438.79	32.13	48766.13
47	48766.13	406.38	438.79	32.40	48733.73
48	48733.73	406.11	438.79	32.67	48701.05
49	48701.05	405.84	438.79	32.94	48668.11

"current" dollars in order to save "future" dollars. "Future" dollars, because of inflation, will be worth less than "current" dollars. So your course of action really depends on your personal financial goals as well as the interest rate on your mortgage and market interest rates. As will be discussed in Chapter 5, prepayment of your mortgage is *one way* to invest discretionary funds effectively. So don't start to prepay your mortgage until you read Chapter 5.

As a final note to this section, we suggest that any prepayments be made by separate check and the cancelled checks stored in case a discrepancy should arise. We also would caution that by reducing the interest you pay during the life of the loan, you are also reducing the amount of your tax writeoffs. Prepayment, however, is certainly an intelligent way to build equity in your home.

The U.S. Department of Housing and Urban Development provides information on many aspects of home purchasing, maintenance, and protection. Most are free and available by writing to the U.S. Superintendent of Documents, Washington, DC. See Chapter 9 for more information.

LET'S SUM UP

The first and probably most important step you can take toward financial independence is owning your home. A home provides a secure financial foundation for any future investments you might wish to make. After purchasing your home, you will need to buy homeowner's insurance to cover any loss by fire, theft, or liability. You also may want to purchase sufficient life insurance to enable your heirs to pay off the mortgage in the event of your death, as well as meet other income needs. In the next chapter we will take a look at your insurance needs and also at how to maximize your coverage at minimum cost.

3

INSURING YOUR FUTURE

A life insurance salesman was standing beside a tractor trying to sell a policy to the farmer. The farmer looked down and said, "No, I want no life insurance—when I die I want it to be a sad day for everyone."

The next important step toward meeting your financial goals is to acquire the insurance coverage you need to maintain your standard of living in the event of death, disability, or other financial catastrophe. Although this chapter certainly isn't meant to be a text on insurance, it will provide some basic guidelines to help you get the insurance you need at minimum cost.

In this chapter we'll take a look at these important points:

- Minimizing the cost of homeowner's and automobile insurance by taking advantage of deductibles and discounts
- Providing the right kind of life insurance at the lowest cost
- Selecting an insurance agent

Insurance, after all, provides you with protection against losses you couldn't afford to pay out of pocket. In other words, insurance keeps you and your family from losing what you already have. Giving thought to the following three guidelines will help you get the best insurance value for your dollar.

1. *Make sure that your basic insurance covers all those risks you likely will incur.*

2. *Determine how much you can afford to lose in each risk category* (your home, vacation home, automobile, furniture, clothing, and special belongings such as jewelry or cameras), and take *deductibles* up to that amount. For instance, if you were to have an automobile accident which is your fault, could you afford to pay the first $100, $200, $500, or maybe even $2,000 worth of repair costs? If you could afford $500 out-of-pocket for repairs, a deductible in this amount could save you a considerable amount on your annual premium.

3. Consider the *maximum possible liability* you might incur and plan to carry insurance to cover that amount. If, for example, you are at fault in a multiple-car collision, would $20,000 really be enough *property*

damage coverage? We hardly think so. Probably $100,000 would be a realistic amount.

CHOOSING AN INSURANCE AGENT

Selecting the right agent is the first step in planning a sound insurance program to cover your home, automobile, business (if you own one), and your life. The selection of the right insurance agent is every bit as important as selecting the right attorney or accountant.

Not surprisingly, however, many people simply rely on friendship in making this critical decision. This may be fine in some cases, but you need to have unemotional, objective advice in selecting insurance. You also want someone who thinks the needs of the "little person" are just as important as those of the wealthier client. You need to be able to call upon your insurance agent on a regular basis—at least once a year—without fear that you might be "intruding" on his or her time.

When you finally select the agent you feel is right for you, give him or her *all* of your insurance business. The only exception to this rule would be group life insurance available through your employer or union or trade association at a lower cost than your agent could provide. Always check these sources of life insurance, as they are often less expensive than policies available from local agents. By letting your agent handle as much of your insurance as possible, you provide an incentive for looking after your needs. You might also receive some discounts on premiums, if, for example, you use the same insurance carrier for your homeowner's and automobile insurance.

Although we advocate the use of one agent, you may find that a single agent will not be able to offer the lowest price on every type of insurance you require. We believe the advantages of using a single agent outweigh the possible savings you might realize by dealing with several agents for several areas of coverage.

HOMEOWNER'S INSURANCE

Homeowner's insurance basically is a combination of fire, theft, and various kinds of liability insurance. The fire and theft portions provide you with benefits in the event you suffer a material loss. The liability

Homeowner's Insurance

portion protects you from lawsuits if someone should become injured on your property.

How much coverage do you need? To put it most simply, *you need enough insurance to cover the full replacement cost of your home and the replacement cost of your furnishings in the event of loss by fire or theft.* Note that you need replacement coverage for both the *dwelling and contents.* Since your policy lists these coverages separately, you may need to make two changes to your present coverage, not just one. Unfortunately, *many people do not have this essential replacement protection*—a fact that can lead to a great deal of sorrow and misfortune if a claim ever has to be filed!

Let's explore this problem. Suppose you purchased a home a few years ago for $60,000. At that time you took out a $50,000 homeowner's policy *based on the fair market value of the structure,* not including the value of the land, and an additional $25,000 for the furnishings and other personal property. (Normally the coverage for contents, excluding cars, pets, and so on, is one half the coverage on your home.) You have a small fire resulting in about $10,000 damage to the structure. You submit your claim, and the insurance company offers you only $5,000 for your misfortune.

"What's going on here?" you protest. The problem is simply that the insurance company determined that it would take $100,000 to *replace* the home at today's building costs (this, by the way, is not the fair market price, which is usually lower than the replacement cost.) Since your current coverage was for only 50 percent of the *replacement cost,* you probably would collect only 50 percent of the claim amount, or $5,000. *In order for you to recover the full amount of the loss* (up to the coverage limit), *you would need coverage at least equal to 80 percent of the replacememt value of your home,* or $80,000 in this example. This percentage, by the way, may vary from one insurance company to another, and so you should be sure to check with your insurance agent for specifics.

Expanding on our example, let's now suppose that the fire destroyed that fancy console television set you bought for $700.00 two years ago. You figure, "No problem, I have $25,000 coverage on the furnishings." You place your claim with the insurance company, and they offer you only $350.00.

You may balk, but after all, what would *you* pay for a used television set. The lesson is clear. Unless you have *full-replacement coverage* on your *scheduled and unscheduled property*, you will recover only the "fair market value of your possessions." Scheduled property would include large-ticket items such as a fur coat and jewelry. Unscheduled property is everything else, such as furnishings, clothing and appliances. Standard homeowner's policies normally do not fully cover unscheduled property, unless you have full-replacement cost coverage. In addition, there is a limit of $500 or $1,000 for loss of *all* jewelry and a similar limit for the loss of *all* furs. Coverage for such scheduled property will be discussed shortly.

Full-replacement coverage of unscheduled property, which typically would cost only an extra $30 to $50 a year, assures you *full replacement value,* even if the price of your furnishings, clothing, and other personal effects has gone up since the property was purchased. If, for example, it now cost $800 to replace the TV set that originally cost $700, you would receive $800 if you have full-replacement value coverage.

Now suppose your home burned down completely. In this instance, you would need insurance with *guaranteed replacement coverage. This coverage would insure replacement of the home even though the replacement cost may exceed the fair market value.* Most policies do *not* provide for guaranteed replacement coverage.

How would you determine the replacement value? One way is to use a simple replacement-cost estimating guide, such as the one developed by the E. H. Boeckh Division of American Appraisal Associates, Inc. Many insurance agents provide this to their customers without charge.

To use the estimator, you first prepare an inventory of the number of rooms, fireplaces, storage areas, areas, and so forth in your home. You then consult the estimator to see which of several categories of homes most closely resembles yours (tract home, custom-built, older home). Tables are provided to determine the basic replacement cost. Finally, an adjustment using your zip code is made to compensate for regional differences in construction costs.

The final figure is the replacement cost for your home. This, of course, is the figure on which you would base the amount of your insurance coverage. Remember again that laws vary from state to state, so be sure to contact your agent to determine the actual replacement-cost coverage you would need.

To give you an example, one of our clients had $80,000 coverage on her home. Based on recent sales in her neighborhood, she felt that her home would sell for $95,000, with $15,000 of that amount allocated for

Homeowner's Insurance

the value of the land. Using the estimator, the client found that the actual replacement cost of the home was about $106,000. She then increased her coverage from $80,000 to $106,000.

Bear in mind that *a real estate agent will appraise your home and property for resale purposes. Insurance appraisers, on the other hand, are interested in the replacement value of the home and its contents.* The market value of the land is irrelevant for insurance purposes. Furthermore, the value used to determine your property taxes is completely irrelevant and usually is much less than the replacement value.

A cautionary note: Some homeowner's policies require that you rebuild on the same site if your home is destroyed. Check with your agent to see if you can have the option to rebuild elsewhere or use the insurance proceeds in some other way.

We believe that maintaining sufficient coverage for catastrophic losses is absolutely essential. You pay only a few extra dollars, but the expenditure is worth every penny. In many instances the extra cost can be offset simply by increasing your deductible for fire and theft coverage. Basically, the higher the dedubtible (the amount which is not covered by the insurance carrier in the event of a loss), the lower your premium will be.

After spending some time reviewing the deductible options, one client concluded that she could withstand an initial loss of $500 in the event of fire or theft. Increasing the deductible from $100 to $500 saved her $62.00 a year, or about a 16 percent reduction of the basic homeowner's premium. Of course, if her home were burglarized or damaged by fire, she would *not* collect the first $500 of loss.

We strongly recommend that you consider at least a $500 deductible for both the structure and contents on your policy and also full replacement cost on your home and its contents.

Proving a Loss of Unscheduled Personal Property

Suppose your home is burglarized. How would you determine your loss? Frequently the most difficult problem is knowing exactly what has been taken. You certainly would miss the couch and TV set, but other stolen items could escape your attention for some time.

How do you keep track of your belongings? Take pictures of all the rooms in your house—and don't forget that table saw in the basement and your clothes in the closets! Keep these pictures in your safe deposit box.

If you have a video camera, consider making a tape of your home, including contents of drawers. Again, keep the cassette in your safe deposit box. You can use the audio portion to provide descriptions, such as "eight suits and six pairs of shoes in bedroom closet." Update your pictures or videotape at least once every two years and when you make major purchases, such as new furniture.

You also may want to list your belongings on an inventory form provided by many insurance agents free of charge. Your insurance carrier may still haggle over the price of some items, but pictures and an inventory should put you in a good negotiating position. Of course, having receipts showing purchase prices is also very helpful in establishing replacement value.

If you sustain a loss, contact your insurance agent immediately. If you were burglarized, notify the police immediately. Your insurance agent should be able and willing to advise you on making a claim. If you have a substantial loss, we recommend that you consider contacting a lawyer before placing any claim with your insurance carrier. Your lawyer can check your policy and describe *all* the coverages you have. Then, you can place a claim for *all* your covered losses.

Scheduled Property

As suggested earlier, many homeowner's policies cover stolen jewelry and furs only to the extent of $500 or $1,000, regardless of what the items actually may be worth. If you have valuable jewelry, boats, furs, sterling silver, antiques, paintings, oriental rugs, books, manuscripts, or any other collectibles, you should ask about obtaining either separate policies for these items or endorsements to your regular homeowner's policy. Such policies or endorsements provide schedules for listing individual items and their appraised values—hence the term, "scheduled property." Naturally, an appraisal is needed to establish policy coverage amounts. *Don't forget that an appraisal must be updated periodically.* If you don't know an appraiser, contact the American Society of Appraisers, P.O. Box 17265, Washington, DC 20041.

Other Coverages You May Need

You should always maintain adequate "loss of use" coverage in the event a fire or other loss forces you to rent temporary living quarters. This

Homeowner's Insurance

coverage is frequently called "additional living expense coverage" and is often included in your policy. If you have someone clean your home or cut your lawn, consider obtaining "employer's liability" coverage. Neither of these coverages is expensive. Again, be sure to check with your agent for particulars.

If you own a computer, you should consider insuring the hardware and software. Insurance is also available for data re-creation in the event a power failure destroyed your data files. Also remember to obtain coverage for such home entertainment items as electronic games, VCRs, tape decks, and stereos.

Earthquake and flood insurance should be considered if you live in an area subject to these natural disasters. Your agent can tell you if you are in a vulnerable area. In the case of flood insurance, the cost will depend on your elevation. The cost of flood insurance may be minimized by obtaining a property elevation certificate from a surveyor. One client, who owned a home at the shore, was able to reduce his premium from $300 to $100 by obtaining an elevation certificate showing that his property was on one of the highest spots in the area. In some shore towns, borough engineers will prepare an elevation certificate at a nominal charge. Check with the borough clerk for specific information.

Credit card insurance is also available, although legislation normally limits your liability to a small amount (usually $50.00) in the event your cards are stolen or fraudulently used. In addition, some homeowner's policies provide coverage for fraudulent use of credit cards. You may not be responsible for any fraudulent purchases if you immediately notify the company that issued the credit card. It's wise, therefore, to keep a list of the telephone numbers and your account numbers in the event your cards are stolen.

As a final note, homeowner's insurance may provide for personal losses away from home, although the coverage may be small. If you travel, for example, you may want to ask your insurance agent if your luggage or clothing is protected against theft, loss, or damage.

If you are a tenant, you should carry tenant's insurance. Usually your landlord's policy does not cover any of the contents of the apartment. If you have jewelry, furs, or other valuables, be sure to obtain additional coverage for them, as they are not covered by most tenant's policies.

How much liability insurance should you carry? Unfortunately, American is a "lawsuit happy" society. We strongly advise you to maintain substantial liability coverage as part of your homeowner's policy—a minimum of $100,000 for each occurrence. The added coverage does not increase your premium very much. Also, you should consider the additional liability coverage provided by an Umbrella Liability Insurance Policy, as described in a following section.

Discounts on Homeowner's Policies

As we discussed earlier, *the largest discounts may result from increasing your deductibles.* This applies not only to homeowner's policies, but also to automobile insurance as well. Although your agent may not mention it, the installation of theft and fire deterrence systems may qualify you for a discount from 2 to 20 percent on your premium. For example, having a smoke detector, fire extinguisher and dead bolts on all doors saved one client we know 5 percent. Had he installed a burglar alarm on the windows and doors, with an outside siren, he could have saved an *additional* 5 percent. Connection of these alarms to a central fire or police department would have meant total savings of 15 percent. Adding automatic sprinklers in all areas of your home in conjunction with your fire detection systems could net you a full 20 percent discount. See the discount charge on page 59 provided by one insurance carrier.

If no one smokes in your home, you may be eligible for up to a 10 percent discount on your fire coverage, depending on your carrier. This could mean substantial savings, in addition to the savings mentioned earlier. Note, however, that some carriers do not provide a discount for nonsmokers. It pays to shop around. Incidentally, 15 percent of all building fires are caused by a smoking-related incident. Nonsmoking policy holders have a significantly lower loss rate than those who smoke.

Some of the items we have described will vary from state to state. Moreover, other discounts, such a discount for a new home, may be available. *One company offers a 10 percent credit on homeowner's insurance for insuring both your automobile and your home with them.*

If you haven't had a claim on your homeowner's policy for a year or more, additional credits may be available. One major carrier provides discounts as follows:

If you have no claims for the last	Upon renewal you get a credit of
1 year	2%
2 years	4%
3 years	6%

You don't have to apply for the credit; it's automatic.

Umbrella Liability Insurance

CERTIFICATION OF APPROVED BURGLARY, SPRINKLER OR FIRE ALARM PROTECTIVE DEVICE

Insureds Name_____ Policy Number_____

Dwelling Location_____

I/we have qualified for _____ % premium credit because I/we have taken preventive measures to help safeguard my/our home from the threat of fire or burglary.

DESCRIPTION OF SYSTEMS

A — Fire or Smoke Detector.

B — Local Burglar Alarm installed on all accessible doors and windows and includes an outside bell or siren and is capable of operating off battery power. (complete back of this form)

C — A fire extinguisher.

D — Dead bolt locks on all exterior doors.

E — Fire or burglar alarm reporting either to a central station or fire department and/or police department. (complete back of this form)

F — An approved and properly maintained automatic sprinkler system with sprinklers in all areas including bathrooms, attics, and attached structures.

G — An approved and properly maintained automatic sprinkler system with sprinklers totally or partly omitted in bathrooms, closets, attics, and attached structures and with fire detectors in all omitted areas.

CREDIT THAT APPLIES. CHECK ONE:

☐ A	2%
☐ B	5%
☐ A, C, D	5%
☐ A, B	7%
☐ A, B, C, D	10%
☐ E	10%
☐ A, E	12%
☐ A, C, D, E	15%
☐ F	10%
☐ B, F	15%
☐ E, F	20%
☐ G	5%
☐ B, G	10%
☐ E, G	15%

In applying for this credit, you agree to maintain the system(s) in working order and to notify us promptly of any change made to the system or if it is removed. We agree not to apply a deductible to any theft loss if we are providing credit for a burglar alarm system (B or E) and this system functions as designed at the time of loss.

UMBRELLA LIABILITY INSURANCE

Probably no more than 5 to 10 percent of all homeowners have it. Indeed, probably no more than 10 or 15 percent have even heard of it. But *umbrella personal liability insurance* is probably the best insurance value in America, and the least expensive! If you have good, basic homeowner and automobile liability policies, you can increase your liability coverage to a million dollars or more for only an additional $80 to $120 a year. Umbrella policies also provide coverages not normally included by a homeowner's policy, such as false arrest, wrongful eviction, libel, slander, defamation of character, and invasion of privacy. For those persons having greater liability exposure, such as those with a backyard swimming pool, an umbrella policy is a must!

Umbrella personal liability insurance, sometimes called the personal excess policy is, in our opinion, the *very best insurance value going.* So why haven't you heard about it? Simply because if you deal with four or five different agents, each of them probably figures, "Why bother?" In addition, a carrier may not be willing to write an umbrella policy unless they also provide the homeowner's, automobile, and other related coverages.

If you have taken our earlier advice about selecting the right agent, he or she will *insist* that you protect your assets with umbrella personal liability coverage for a million or more dollars. He or she will also help you determine the maximum deductible you can afford, in addition to providing you with annual updates for inflation. Should you decide not to take out the umbrella policy, the agent may ask you for a letter saying that you don't want the coverage.

The principle here is a very simple one—the greater your assets, the more you need a comprehensive, personal insurance program.

AUTOMOBILE INSURANCE

Automobile policies differ widely from state to state. Accordingly, we limit our recommendations to the following six important areas:

1. *Carry sufficient liability insurance*—at least $300,000 per person. We also recommend including the automobile liability as part of your umbrella coverage so that the limit on liability is raised to $1,000,000 or more.

2. *Carry sufficient property damage insurance.* We recommend $100,000 minimum coverage.

3. *Consider a $500 deductible on your collision insurance.* This will save you a substantial amount. For example, most collision insurance is based on a $200 deductible. One example of discounts for higher deductibles is shown at the top of page 61.

Thus, if your $200 deductible rate is $300, the rate for a $500 deductible would be $207 (.65 [$300] + $12 = $207).

| | Multiply $200 | |
For a Deductible of	Deductible Rate by	And Add
$ 500	.65	$12
1,000	.50	18
1,500	.45	19
2,000	.40	21

  4. *Consider at least a $200 deductible for comprehensive coverage.*

  5. *Before you purchase a new car, check the policy costs with your agent.* Find out if there are discounts for smaller cars. Also, some cars are prime targets for thieves and therefore may be subject to higher premiums. Of course, higher priced cars are more expensive to insure, mainly because of higher repair costs. Insurance agents use a "Vehicle Services Rating" to determine insurance premiums. The higher the rating, the more the premium. To show you what we mean, a 1985 Cadillac Eldorado Convertible has a rating of 16, whereas a 1985 two-door Chevette is rated at only six. Surprisingly, a 1985 Subaru four-door GL is rated at 10, whereas the same model for the years 1981–84 is rated at a whopping 18!

  6. Consider using the same insurance carrier for both your automobile and homeowner's coverage. This may lead to a discount on your homeowner's policy, as noted earlier.

If you believe that you need additional help in selecting the automobile coverage you need, your local Bar Association usually can recommend an attorney. He or she can provide free or low-cost information regarding automobile insurance coverage and the various options available under your state insurance laws.

LIFE INSURANCE

  "The reason why worry kills more people than work is that more people worry than work."

In looking at life insurance, ask yourself these three questions:

  1. What kind should I buy (term, whole life, universal, variable)?
  2. How much do I need?
  3. How much can I afford?

What kind of life insurance should you purchase? At this juncture, we recommend that you consider life insurance primarily for the protection it can provide you and your spouse rather than as a means for investing funds. Furthermore, the decision to purchase life insurance should be made within your overall financial plan. As we discuss in the following sections, whole life, universal life, and variable life provide both life insurance coverage and investment of funds. Maybe you already believe that investing funds using universal life is in your best interest. But before you make any decision to purchase insurance, you should read Chapters 4 through 7, which outline other financial planning techniques and investment options. This is in line with our recommendation in Chapter 2 to postpone prepaying your mortgage until you have established your financial goals and have considered other investment options.

There are five basic kinds of life insurance, although various insurance companies have numerous names for the policies they sell. The main features of each kind are listed below.

Group Life Insurance

- Group life is normally provided by your employer as a fringe benefit.
- It is normally provided in amounts that are a multiple of your salary. Typically, the multiple is one to three times your annual salary.
- When you retire, it usually decreases substantially or is cancelled.
- As your salary increases, frequently the coverage also increases.
- There may be "extra" coverage if you are injured on the job or while travelling for your employer.
- If you leave your employer and want to retain the insurance coverage, you may have to convert the group coverage to whole life coverage. The whole life premium will depend on your age and can be very expensive.

Term Life Insurance

- Term life is pure insurance protection and does not build cash value.
- It is the least costly, especially when you are young.

Life Insurance

- Its function is to provide a specified dollar level of protection for a specified period of time at a predetermined, fixed premium.
- Some term policies can be renewed after they expire.
- Many term policies can be converted to whole life without taking a medical exam.

Although in prior years most term policies expired at age 65, term insurance now can be purchased until age 95, but the premiums would be very costly, especially at older ages. Premiums for a fixed-dollar, term policy, which we describe in the following section, increase substantially from year to year.

Term policies are inexpensive because only a small percentage of the policies are ever paid. Most either expire or are allowed to lapse by the policyholder. Some term policies provide for a fixed dollar amount of insurance, with the premiums increasing each year. For example, one agent provided us with the following rates for a person 35 years of age who does not smoke. The policy is in the amount of $100,000.

Note the two columns, "Current" and "Guaranteed Maximum." The "Current" column indicates the expected annual premium. This particular insurance company guarantees the current premium for the first three years of the policy's life. After that, the premium is guaranteed *not* to exceed the "Guaranteed Maximum."

TABLE 3-1 Annual Premiums for Term Life Policy

Age	Current	Guaranteed Maximum
35	$ 144.00	$ 261.00
36	172.00	271.00
37	194.00	284.00
38	202.00	299.00
39	213.00	319.00
40	225.00	340.00
41	238.00	364.00
42	254.00	391.00
43	270.00	420.00
44	289.00	454.00
45	307.00	488.00
50	435.00	741.00
55	698.00	1,203.00
60	865.00	1,628.00
65	1,386.00	2,699.00

The premium for this policy contains a "waiver of premium." This means that the life insurance company will waive your premiums if you are unable to work at any job because of sickness or injury, and your disability has lasted six months and begins prior to age 60.

Some term policies have a fixed premium, with the coverage decreasing each year. These are called *decreasing term* policies. For example, the authors were provided with the following schedule for a fixed premium policy on a 35-year-old nonsmoker. The initial coverage is $100,000 and the premium is $247.00 per year. Although the coverage decreases from year to year, the changes are shown in five-year intervals:

Age	Coverage
35	$100,000
40	86,700
45	70,000
50	53,300
55	36,700
60–65	20,000

Term policies are available for specific periods to provide for specific coverage, such as mortgage credit life insurance and automobile credit life insurance. For example, you might want to purchase decreasing term life insurance to pay off a mortgage should you or your spouse die. Such policies, which include the premiums as part of your monthly mortgage payment, are frequently sold by lending institutions. We recommend purchasing this kind of policy, but we advise you to shop around for the best value. Ask the lending institution for a copy of your mortgage amortization schedule (see Chapter 2). Take the schedule to one or more insurance agents to obtain quotes for the premiums to cover the outstanding principal on the loan. In addition, consider other forms of term coverage, such as nondecreasing term available from your union or employer. Even though a nondecreasing policy from your union or employer might provide *more* coverage than you really need in the future, you may actually pay less for it than you would for a decreasing term policy offered by a lending institution or an insurance agent. Shop around—term policies are frequently available from unions, employers, professional associations, trade associations, and pension funds at very low rates.

Whole Life Insurance

- Whole life has been largely replaced by universal life and variable life.
- Whole life combines permanent life insurance and a long-range savings plan.
- The premiums stay the same for the life of the policy.
- Premiums are *higher* than for the same coverage of term life insurance.
- Part of the premium pays for the life insurance, in addition to sales commissions and administrative expenses. The remainder is invested in the policy to build cash value.
- You can surrender the policy for its current cash value at any time. You should bear in mind, however, that *the cash value will be minimal until the policy has been in effect for many years.*

You can usually borrow against a whole life policy at a low rate of interest. This can prove very profitable if interest rates are high and there is at least a 2 percent difference between the loan rate on your policy and the rate you can obtain on a risk-free investment such as a Certificate of Deposit (discussed in Chapter 4). Note, however, that under the Tax Reform Act of 1986, the interest deductibility of such loans is being phased out if the proceeds are used for personal purposes. (See Chapter 1 for more details on the tax deductibility of interest.) Note also that under the Tax Reform Act of 1986 the interest from any investments, such as from Certificates of Deposit, is still subject to tax. Therefore, the desirability of borrowing against your life insurance policy will decrease. Consult your accountant or tax advisor before borrowing against your life insurance policy.

The rate of return on the invested portion of the whole life policy tends to be low—4 to 8 percent, sometimes even less. However, some whole life policies offer annual dividends, which can help to reduce the premium payment. And, importantly, whole life policies do not terminate at age 65—a fact that should be considered if you need coverage after this age.

Universal Life

Universal life provides a combination of insurance and *tax-free buildup of savings.* The amount of this buildup depends on the rate of return the insurance company is able to obtain. This will vary from period to period, and so it is not possible to know what the surrender value of the policy will be in the future. At a 10.25 percent return, for example, a $100,000 policy designed for a 35-year-old nonsmoker would have a surrender value of $45,589 at age 65. By contrast, an 8.75 percent return would yield a surrender value of only $28,014 at age 65. The actual return may be lower than the rates shown in the examples provided by agents selling the policies.

The surrender value depends on three factors:

1. *The amount of premium you pay.* Normally, each premium payment goes into what the insurance companies call a "cash value account." Interest is credited on a monthly basis. Also on a monthly basis, the insurance carrier deducts administrative and mortality-rate charges from the cash value account to cover the cost of insurance and any benefit riders you select. During the first year, additional expenses may also be deducted. The larger the premium you pay, the more you accumulate in your cash value account.

2. *The rate of return obtained by the insurance carrier on your premiums.* The rate is the *critical determinant.* If you believe that the insurance company's investment managers can outperform other kinds of investments, such as those discussed in following chapters, you may want to mix insurance with investments in your overall portfolio using universal life.

3. *The length of time the policy has been in force.* Since the surrender value depends largely on the amount of premium you pay, it is possible, after a number of years, that the death benefit may exceed the face amount of the policy.

Universal life is designed to be a tax shelter. Suppose, for example, you paid $30,000 in premiums over a period of years, and the surrender value of the policy has increased to $50,000. If you surrendered the policy and took the $50,000, you would have to pay taxes only on the difference between the surrender value and the premiums paid—$20,000 in this case.

Generally, premiums may be paid in either one large amount ($5,000 to $500,000), called a "single-payment life insurance policy," to purchase lifetime coverage or in smaller yearly or monthly premiums.

In addition, the premiums may be flexible, permitting changes in coverage as your need for insurance coverage changes.

A policy holder usually may borrow nearly all of the policy's surrender value. Usually the interest rate on the loan approximates the rate that the insurance company is obtaining on your premiums. As a result, the interest rate on a loan may vary from period to period. Some policies, however, provide for guaranteed loan rates. The same limitations on the tax deductibility of interest described for loans against whole life policies also apply to universal and other life policies.

Variable Life Insurance

Variable life is a hybrid of universal life. The premiums may be invested at your discretion in fixed-income securities such as bonds, or they can be invested in stocks, money-market funds (described in Chapter 4), or some combination of these. If you specify, for example, that the funds are to be invested in stocks, you may have a greater or lesser surrender value depending on the performance of the stock market over the years. In addition, the premiums are generally fixed rather than variable and may be a single payment.

Although the death benefit will not decrease below the amount originally purchased, it may increase and subsequently decrease depending on the investment experience of the accounts in which the premiums (less expenses) are invested. Thus the cash value of the policy increases or decreases daily depending on investment experience.

If you decide to mix insurance with investment, using universal or variable life, try to limit yourself to those insurance companies with an A+ rating from the A.M. Best Co., an independent rating service. Ask the sales agent to obtain the rating for you, or you may want to contact your state's insurance commissioner. He or she should also be able to provide you with a particular company's rating.

We also recommend that you contact the National Insurance Consumer Organization (NICO) at 121 North Payne St., Alexandria, Virginia, 22314, once you have identified a particular policy you think will meet your combined investment and insurance needs. For a modest fee of $25.00, they will provide you with an unbiased report on the actual rates of return after costs and commissions have been figured in. Their services also may be helpful if you want to rank proposed policies based on their rates of return. Finally, *Consumer Reports* magazine periodically provides valuable information on universal and other forms of life insurance.

HOW MUCH INSURANCE DO YOU NEED?

"The sure way to mishandle a problem is to avoid facing up to it."

The amount of life insurance you need depends on numerous factors, many of which are described in the paragraphs that follow. As we noted earlier, the decision to purchase life insurance should be made within your overall financial plan. So postpone changing your coverage until you have read Chapters Four through Seven.

1. *If you don't need the insurance, don't buy it.* Yes, if you are age 22, you can buy a great deal of life insurance for a small premium. But if you aren't supporting a family, maybe you really don't need all that insurance. Just because something is cheap doesn't make it a good buy.

But if you do foresee the need for insurance, this could be a good time to purchase, especially if you have a family medical history of diabetes, kidney disease, or similar diseases. Specifically, one agent suggested a $100,000 policy for a 22-year-old person. The premium would be $795 per year for five years, after which the policy would be paid up. The death benefit is $100,000 to age 65 and $50,000 afterwards.

2. *If you are looking for a job or changing your position, check on your potential employer's group life insurance plan.* Some employers may not provide any, while others may offer three to four times your base pay in life coverage as a fringe benefit. Moreover, some employer pension plans include a lump-sum death benefit payable to your beneficiary.

3. *Consider purchasing decreasing term life insurance* so that your mortgage and car (and boat) loans would be paid off in the event you die or your spouse dies. Shop around for the least expensive kind of term insurance to provide this coverage. It can provide real security to your spouse by eliminating mortgage and other monthly payments. We think it is very important that you have sufficient life insurance to pay off your mortgage as well as any automobile and other consumer loans.

4. *If you are single, without children,* and your employer provides some life insurance coverage, you probably don't need any more. If you have "extra" money to invest, we recommend that you do not put it in life insurance. Consider the options discussed in Chapters Four through Seven before making a decision.

5. *If you are a childless married couple* with a spouse who is

How Much Insurance Do You Need?

employed, or expects to be employed, and your employer provides insurance coverage, consider buying only the additional term insurance coverage outlined in Paragraph Three. You probably don't need any more insurance. Again, invest any "extra" money.

6. *If you have children* and are employed, or have been employed, and you die, your spouse likely would receive survivor's benefits for the children until they reach 18 years of age. Currently, when a child reaches 18, the benefit checks stop, unless he or she remains unmarried, is disabled, or is a full-time elementary or secondary school student.

If your spouse does not work or has only a limited income, he or she also would receive survivor's benefits until the youngest child is 16. *Social Security Survivor Benefits* can be a real help in meeting a surviving spouse's needs, including those of the children. Obviously, these dollars will go further if you don't have mortgage or automobile loan payments. This is why we recommend the coverage described in Paragraph 3.

Before purchasing any life insurance, contact your Social Security office to obtain an estimate of the benefits for your children and your spouse if you should die.

7. *Insurance for women is just as important as it is for men,* especially if both spouses are employed. The amounts of coverage needed may vary, but a surviving spouse, regardless of sex, with children almost always needs insurance benefits. Discounts may be available if both you and your spouse purchase insurance from the same carrier.

8. *Insurance for children should be considered.* You may want to maintain at least a minimal policy which would cover funeral expenses.

9. Recognize that if you die, your spouse may remarry. Naturally, you can't be sure of this, but the probability of remarriage is *very high,* especially if the surviving spouse is a man. Generally, if a surviving spouse remarries, his or her insurance needs will decrease.

10. We understand that no two people may have exactly the same needs or wants, but the following steps should help most of you determine your life insurance needs:

   a. Determine how much after-tax income your family will need each year until your *youngest child* completes high school or, if appropriate, college.
   b. Subtract the mortgage and automobile payments (*we assume you have insurance coverage as outlined in Paragraph 3*), your spouse's after-tax income, any Social Security benefits or other benefits, and any income from current investments. The result

represents the "additional" after-tax income your family will need each year to maintain their current standard of living.

c. Since the amount of additional after-tax income your family will need will change from year to year, *compute the average amount they will need to simplify calculations.*

d. Multiply the average amount determined in step "c" by the "Factor" shown in the Table 3-2 which corresponds to the number of years remaining until your youngest child graduates from high school or college. For example, if your family will require an additional income averaging $600 per month ($7,200) per year, then you need about $72,000 of life insurance ($7,200 × 10.0 = $72,000).

e. Having determined the amount of coverage you require, add

TABLE 3-2 Present Value Factors

Age of Youngest Child	Years Income Needed	Factor (based on 3% rate of return on invested proceeds)*
21	1	1.0
20	2	1.9
19	3	2.8
18	4	3.7
17	5	4.6
16	6	5.4
15	7	6.2
14	8	7.0
13	9	7.8
12	10	8.5
11	11	9.3
10	12	10.0
9	13	10.6
8	14	11.3
7	15	11.9
6	16	12.6
5	17	13.2
4	18	13.8
3	19	14.3
2	20	14.9
1	21	15.4
Just Born	22	15.9

*A 3 percent return is used to avoid the effects of inflation. Your actual return probably will be considerably greater, perhaps 9 percent. But if you obtain a 9 percent rate, inflation probably will be in the 3 to 4 percent range, leaving you with a *real*, after-tax return of approximately 3 percent.

$10,000 to cover funeral and other expenses. Then, subtract any life insurance coverage provided by your employer. The difference is the amount of insurance you should consider purchasing (in addition to the coverage described in Paragraph 3). *Note, of course, that if you want to provide for your spouse and your children for a longer period of time, you would need additional coverage.*

If you have difficulty following the steps just described and are not sure how much coverage you need, we recommend calling an accounting or finance professor at a local college. He or she should be able to assist you at minimal cost.

11. *Your income and expenses will change from year to year.* Also, you may have children, change jobs, or move away. Accordingly, you should review your insurance needs at least every three years and whenever a major event takes place, such as the birth of a child.

12. *Investing insurance proceeds wisely is just as important as purchasing the right amount.* Insurance proceeds can be squandered very quickly. Refer to the section on trusts in Chapter 8 for some ideas on managing insurance proceeds.

13. *Not smoking and maintaining normal weight can reduce your policy premiums.* So called "nonsmoker's build" rates, which typically require that the insured has not smoked cigarettes for one year or more and is not substantially overweight, are significantly lower than rates for those who smoke and are overweight.

LET'S SUM UP

Determining the insurance coverage you need and the least expensive way to purchase it will take some time, but it may be the most valuable time you will ever spend. You can maximize your coverage and minimize your costs by following the guidelines in this chapter.

We have introduced two ways to invest money: Prepaying your mortgage and purchasing universal or variable life insurance. Understandably, you may be anxious to get started in an investment program. But we advise postponing any investment decisions until you have established financial goals and have evaluated the investment alternatives described in subsequent chapters. So let's forge ahead to look at other areas you need to explore to build financial independence.

4

INVESTMENT ALTERNATIVES

"If only God would give me a clear sign—like making a large deposit in my name at a Swiss bank!"

woody allen

Now you are in a position to start planning to invest for your financial independence. Our goal in this and the following three chapters is to provide you with the information you need to plan investment strategies and select those investments which will help you achieve your financial goals. We will describe the various investment alternatives available to you and indicate where each may fit into your portfolio.

This chapter will examine:

- The 12 classes of investments available to you
- The savings opportunities offered by banks and other savings institutions
- Minimizing risk by investing in government securities
- Investing in common stock and other corporate securities
- Mutual funds
- Tax-deferred annuities that can enhance your investment program

AN OVERVIEW—TWELVE TYPES OF INVESTMENTS

You have at least 12 broad classes of possible investments available to you. Each has particular characteristics which can add to its attractiveness depending on your financial goals. We list the various classes of investments briefly here; the most important ones are described in more detail in this and the following three chapters.

1. *Banks and savings institutions*. Banks and other savings institutions offer a wide range of investment opportunities, including passbook or statement savings accounts, money market accounts, and certificates of deposit (CDs). These investments are described in this chapter.

2. *Your own home*. Fixing up, adding to, or even purchasing a more expensive home in a good location can be an excellent investment and add to your living comfort as well. In addition, it can offer substantial Federal income tax savings. If, for instance, you sell your larger home after you reach the age of 55, the first $125,000 in appreciation is free

from any Federal income tax. You might then purchase a smaller home and invest the difference to provide additional income during your retirement years.

3. *Federal government and government guaranteed.* The U.S. Treasury offers several short- and long-term obligations, including Treasury Bills, Treasury Notes, Series EE and Series HH Bonds, and Treasury Bonds. Other government guaranteed securities are also available. These investments are discussed in this chapter.

4. *State, county, and municipal governments and authorities.* States and other governments issue bonds which, as a group, are called *municipal bonds*. Municipal bonds have a particular advantage as investments; the interest may not be subject to Federal income taxation or to state tax. Municipal bonds are so important to investors that two sections in Chapter Six are devoted to municipal bonds and a special type of municipal bond investment called a Municipal Bond Unit Trust.

5. *Corporations.* Corporations sell a number of securities, such as common stock, preferred stock, and bonds. Common stock, in particular, is a very popular vehicle for investment. Corporate investments are described in this chapter. Since corporate common stock is so important to many investors, we have devoted a major portion of Chapter 6 to explaining the system we use to select common stocks for our portfolios.

6. *Commodities.* Gold, silver, and platinum represent three familiar commodities available to you. Commodity trading is a highly specialized field of investment. We recommend commodity trading only for the most sophisticated investors and therefore do not discuss it in this book.

7. *Real Estate.* Rental real estate has and continues to be a very popular investment for those who want to become personally involved with the management of their investments. Unlike most other types of investments, rental real estate is unique in that it affords a high degree of financial leverage. That is, you can purchase real estate with a relatively small down payment. Investment in rental real estate is discussed in Chapter 7.

8. *Your own business.* Many people ignore this potentially very rewarding and profitable type of investment. Our experience indicates that a part-time business operated out of your own home, which takes advantage of your interests, skills or a hobby, may be one of the best investment alternatives available. Numerous business opportunities exist which can bring you profit and joy. In Chapter 7, we look at the advantages of investing in your own business.

9. *Collectibles, antiques, and related items.* Those who profit from coins, stamps, antiques, and other collectibles are capitalizing on special expertise. You can find many books dealing with the specifics of each type of collectible. Personal experience and knowledge, combined with good business sense, are essential for success. Since relatively few people truly invest in collectibles and trade them for a profit, we don't discuss collectibles in this book. This should not discourage you, however. If you have the expertise, capitalize on it!

10. *Mutual funds.* You can choose dozens of mutual funds—companies that manage portfolios of stocks, bonds, and other securities. Rather than purchase individual securities, you may purchase shares of a mutual fund, which, in effect, gives you partial ownership of a large number of securities. Mutual funds represent a very popular way to invest in securities and are discussed in this chapter.

11. *Tax-deferred annuities and related investments.* You may want to consider a wide variety of tax-deferred investments. For example, you may be able to make additional tax-deferred contributions to your pension fund. An individual retirement account may provide a means for postponing payment taxes on current earnings. We discuss these possibilities in Chapter 5.

Through universal and variable life insurance policies, insurance companies offer ways to invest funds and to defer the tax on the income earned. These were discussed in Chapter 3. Insurance companies also offer tax-deferred annuities, which are discussed in this chapter.

12. *Repayment of debt.* One of the easiest and least risky of all investments is the early repayment of outstanding debts—your home mortgage, in particular. We briefly discussed mortgage prepayment in Chapter 2 and will examine it in more detail in Chapter 5.

INVESTMENTS OFFERED BY BANKS AND SAVINGS INSTITUTIONS

You probably are most familiar with the savings plans offered by banks and other savings institutions. As a child, you probably had a passbook savings account, and millions of people do today.

Most people view savings in banks and other savings institutions as essentially risk free. That is, they believe there is very little *risk of default,* and therefore they will not lose their money even if the savings institution should fail. Signs are posted on the front door and inside of participating institutions telling you that your account is insured up to $100,000 by the Federal Deposit Insurance Corporation or the Federal Savings and Loan Insurance Corporation. Generally, in fact, there is very little risk of default involved. But with the increasing number of bank and savings and loan failures in recent years, the deposit insurance systems have been under a lot of pressure. We therefore advise you to avoid putting all of your assets in one savings institution. Diversify! Spread your savings among several institutions.

Banks and other savings institutions offer a variety of savings programs. Those of primary importance are listed here.

Passbook or statement savings accounts offer great flexibility by permitting easy withdrawal of funds in person or by mail and sometimes by telephone transfer to your checking account (or NOW Account) at the same bank. Passbook savings accounts usually pay a very low rate of interest; some don't pay any interest if the balance falls below a minimum such as $100. Statement savings usually pay a somewhat higher rate. In some instances, charges may be connected with the statement savings accounts. For example, one bank we are familiar with charges a $1.00 monthly fee if your account balance falls below $100.

We generally discourage the use of passbook or statement savings accounts because they pay such low rates of interest. You normally will receive about the same rate on a negotiable order of withdrawal (NOW) account (discussed in Chapter 1). Many people view such interest-bearing checking accounts as the place to deposit their paychecks and the vehicle for paying their bills. You certainly can use a NOW account, however, to accumulate funds until you are ready to transfer them to other types of investments.

Certificates of Deposit (CDs) have the advantage of paying higher rates of interest than passbook or savings accounts. But there is a price; you give up access to your money. Generally, *if you withdraw funds from a CD before it matures, you will incur a substantial interest penalty.* In addition, the depository institution may not permit you to withdraw your money unless you can demonstrate an emergency or a hardship. If necessary, you may borrow using the CD as collateral. Institutions issuing the CDs usually charge about 2 percent more interest on the loan than the CD is yielding. So, if you had a CD which yielded 6 percent, you likely could borrow against it at about 8 percent. CDs therefore should be used only if you are reasonably certain that you won't need your money until the CD matures.

Likewise, you should avoid long-term CDs if you believe that interest rates are likely to increase substantially. If you purchase an 8 percent certificate with a five-year maturity, and interest rates increase to 10 percent, you won't be able to shift to 10 percent without incurring a penalty, if indeed you can shift at all. Thus, CDs do have some *"market risk,"* in that you may not be able to take advantage of current market yields because you are effectively "locked into" a lower-yielding certificate. Market risk results at least in part from changes in the rate of inflation. Generally, if the rate of inflation increases, interest rates are likely to increase.

Maturities of CDs generally range from six months to several years, with the interest rate fixed for that period. It should be noted, however, that interest rates vary among savings institutions, so it pays to call for rates at several institutions before purchasing a CD. As noted in Chapter 1, *always compare the effective interest rate (yield)* when doing comparison shopping for interest rates. Usually, the longer the maturity, the higher the rate of interest paid. Therefore, some people purchase certificates with maturities of five or more years. This is risky, since, as noted already, access to your money may be limited and you could be locked into a low rate if interest rates should increase.

When you shop for high interest rates, you may want to use out-of-town savings institutions. Before you consider saving away from home, send for the 35-page booklet, "How Safe Is Your Money?" available for $1.00 from *100 Highest Yields,* P.O. Box 088888, North Palm Beach, FL 33408.

CDs have become a very popular form of investment, especially when a person wants to avoid risk and knows that the money will not be needed for a period of time. Interest may be payable to you by check, monthly, quarterly or semiannually, or you may let the interest accrue. You receive the same interest rate on accrued interest as you do on your original deposit. Many people put their IRA deposits in CDs and let the interest accrue. *CDs represent a safe way to save for the future and require minimal management.*

Money market deposit accounts are similar to statement savings accounts in that you have easy access to your money. Money market deposit accounts pay higher rates of interest but may limit the numbers of withdrawals each month. The interest rate varies from month to month, or more frequently, and generally is lower than the rates paid on even short-term CDs. Moreover, rates vary among banks. (*Barron's Financial Weekly* provides a survey of top-paying banks. See Chapter 9 for details.) You make a tradeoff, however. With a CD you give up access to your money (except by paying a penalty) and receive a higher rate of interest. Money market deposit accounts offer easy access to your money.

We view money market deposit accounts as a good place to put short-term savings. If you are saving for a new car or a home, for example, a money market deposit account is an excellent place to save your money. Moreover, if you believe that the general level of interest rates is going to increase, you can use a money market deposit account as a place to "park" your money until interest rates increase and other investments, such as CDs, become attractive. We would not recommend using a money market deposit account as a way to save for an extended period of time. The funds might be better placed in CDs, bonds, or other long-term securities.

IRA variable interest accounts are especially useful for those who want to contribute to an IRA but don't have sufficient funds to make their annual contribution all at one time. For example, you could contribute a few hundred dollars at the start of the year and more later. Then, when you have accumulated enough to purchase a CD, you could "roll over" your IRA deposit into the CD. Similar periodic contributions could be made to an IRA invested in a mutual fund, for example, so you do have more than one choice if you don't have all of your annual contribution available at one time.

IRA variable interest accounts generally pay higher rates of interest than money-market deposit accounts but lower rates than many CDs. *We view variable-interest IRA accounts as useful for accumulating IRA deposits during a year but probably a poor choice if you are looking for a place to deposit your IRA funds for a long period.* If you want to maintain your IRA in a savings institution, a CD probably would be a better choice. Of course, if you expect interest rates to increase, you might want to park your IRA contributions in an IRA variable-interest account and move them when interest rates increase.

FEDERAL GOVERNMENT SECURITIES

The Federal government offers a wide variety of savings investments. They generally are divided into three types: (1) Series EE and HH Savings Bonds sold through banks; (2) Treasury Bills, Notes and Bonds, which may be purchased directly through the Federal Reserve Banks and stock brokers; (3) government-guaranteed securities sold primarily through stock brokers.

Federal Government Securities

You probably are most familiar with savings bonds. Many people purchase savings bonds through regular payroll deduction plans. This is an "easy" way to save; the money is "gone" before you spend it. This feature of payroll deduction is not unique to savings bonds. You might, for example, make additional contributions to your pension plan through payroll deductions. Thus, savings bonds should be considered on their investment merit rather than as simply an "easy way to save."

Savings bonds and other Federal government obligations offer one particular advantage; *there is no risk of default*. As a consequence, they tend to pay lower rates of interest than bank CDs of similar maturity, for example. As is the case with all other long-term investments, however, Treasury investments, such as Series EE Saving Bonds, do suffer from *inherent market risk* described earlier in this chapter.

Series EE bonds offer some features which make them well worth considering especially if you are saving for retirement or a child's education:

- *They are sold at a discount.* For example, you pay $25 for a bond with a $50 face value. The difference is the interest you receive when the bond matures.
- *Interest is exempt from state and local income tax.*
- *Interest is subject to Federal tax.* The tax may be paid annually or deferred until the bonds are cashed, disposed of, or reach maturity, whichever comes first. If you elect to pay the tax on the interest annually, your election is binding for all presently owned bonds, as well as those acquired subsequently.
- *The stated maturity is ten years, but the actual maturity will vary,* since the interest rate received on bonds is variable after the first five years and fluctuates with the current rate of interest. Thus, Series EE Bonds are risk-free both with respect to default and, after five years, to fluctuations in the market rate of interest. If the general level of interest rates increases, the interest rate on your bond will increase and vice versa.
- *Federal tax on interest received on Series EE Bonds may be deferred further* by exchanging the Series EE bonds for Series HH bonds.
- *They may be redeemed any time after six months or more after purchase.* If you keep the bonds less than five years, the interest rate is quite low. Thus, *Series EE Bonds should be kept at least five years; preferably until maturity.*

Since the Federal tax on Series EE bonds can be deferred until they mature, and you may be able to keep them beyond maturity, they provide a low-risk way to enjoy tax-deferred income. You are limited on the number of years you may keep them and still continue to collect interest, so don't just put your bonds in a drawer and forget them. If you have older savings bonds, check with a local savings institution to be sure that they are still paying interest.

Series HH bonds may not be purchased directly. They may be purchased in exchange for outstanding Series EE bonds. Unlike Series EE bonds, they are sold at face value and pay interest semiannually, with maturity in ten years. Tax on interest from Series HH Bonds must be paid in the year it is received.

Used in conjunction with Series EE bonds, HH bonds are very attractive for retirement savings. Owners of Series EE bonds who have deferred reporting interest may continue to defer such reporting to the taxable year in which the HH bonds received in exchange for the EE bonds are redeemed, disposed of, or reach maturity, whichever comes first. For example, suppose you purchased a $1,000 Series EE bond for $500. At maturity, $500 of interest would have accrued. If you redeemed the bond at that time, you would have to pay the tax on $500 interest. If, however, you exchange the Series EE Bond for a Series HH Bond, you may continue to tax defer the $500 of interest as long as you have the Series HH Bond.

With a little planning, you can exchange your Series EE bonds for Series HH bonds after you retire, when you may have a lower tax rate. You then can use the interest income from the Series HH Bonds to supplement your pension and other retirement income.

Although we suggest you consider the Uniform Gift to Minors Account described in Chapter 5 as a mechanism for saving for a child's college education, Series EE Bonds also should be considered. You may ask friends and relatives to give bonds to a child at birth and at subsequent birthdays and holiday celebrations. With the bonds placed in the child's name, the interest may be taxable to the child either annually or when they are cashed.

But note the following changes resulting from the Tax Reform Act of 1986. If the child is less than 14 years old, net unearned income (which includes interest) in excess of $1,000 per year may be taxed at the parent's marginal tax rate. However, if the child has earned income, a portion of the first $1,000 of unearned income may also be taxed at the parent's marginal tax rate. Thus, if your child is given a substantial number of bonds, you should consult your tax advisor or accountant before electing to pay tax on the interest annually.

Series EE Bonds are very attractive as gifts because they appear to be worth more than they really are. Giving a $100 bond, for example, costs you only $50. They are also very easy to purchase and may simplify gift giving for birthdays and at holiday seasons. Finally, when purchased systematically, they can result in substantial accumulations over an 18-year period. At an average yield of 7 percent, $100 invested in savings bonds *each year* for 18 years will amount to $3,400.

Treasury Bills (T-Bills) are short-term securities, maturing in three, six, or 12 months. They are sold weekly. There is an active "secondary market" for outstanding T-Bills. Thus, if you wanted to purchase a T-Bill maturing in four months, for example, you could do so in the "secondary market" through a stock broker.

Similar to Series EE bonds, T-Bills are sold at a discount—that is, less than their maturity value. The interest is the difference between the amount you receive at maturity and the amount you pay. T-Bills are sold in $10,000 denominations and may be purchased directly through the Federal Reserve Bank or through commercial banks or stock brokers. Since many people do not have $10,000 to invest, they may purchase shares of a money-market mutual fund (described later in this chapter) which purchases T-Bills.

Since T-Bills have virtually no risk of default and are very liquid (you can easily sell a T-Bill prior to maturity), they may pay a lower rate of interest than other short-term securities. A money-market deposit account, for example, which offers as much liquidity and is insured usually would pay a higher rate of interest. Consequently, unless you have a lot of money to invest and want to use T-Bills as a way to diversify your portfolio, we don't recommend them.

Treasury notes and bonds are similar to Treasury bills in that they are direct obligations of the U.S. government and are therefore considered to be risk-free with respect to default. They differ in three ways:

1. *They pay interest semiannually.*
2. *They have longer maturities;* notes mature in two to ten years, while bonds mature in ten to 30 years.
3. *They do entail market risk.*

Notes and bonds are sold in smaller denominations than T-Bills and therefore may be more attractive to a small investor. With some exceptions, they are sold in $1,000 denominations. You may purchase new issues of notes and bonds directly through the Federal Reserve Bank without commission. You also may make purchases through a commercial bank or stock broker (a commission will be charged). Moreover, a very active secondary market exists for these securities, and so you may easily purchase bonds with a short period until maturity or sell bonds prior to their maturity.

Although notes and bonds are risk-free with respect to default, their values do fluctuate as interest rates change. This means that if you want to sell a note or bond prior to maturity, you may receive more or less than you paid for it. If you purchase during a period of low interest rates, and the rates subsequently increase, you may incur a very substantial loss if you sell. Therefore, as noted above, Treasury notes and bonds do entail market risk. Consequently, when interest rates are low, *we recommend purchasing Treasury notes or bonds which are within three or four years of maturity. When interest rates are high, you may want to purchase notes or bonds with longer periods to maturity and "lock in" a higher rate.*

Treasury notes and especially Treasury bonds have a very useful investment function. To understand this you must recognize a particular feature of most corporate bonds, since Treasury bonds compete with corporate bonds. Although corporate bonds pay a higher rate of return than similar maturity Treasury bonds, and therefore may appear preferable even though some risk of default exists, many corporate bonds are "callable." This means that the company issuing the bond may "call in the bonds," literally requiring you to sell the bonds back to the company. This can have very adverse effects on your portfolio, as demonstrated in the following example.

Suppose in a period of inflation, interest rates are up and investment-grade corporate bonds are issued yielding 13 percent, while newly issued Treasury bonds of similar maturity are yielding only 11.5 percent. You choose to purchase some corporate bonds to obtain the higher yield. Two years later inflation has subsided, and the yield on newly issued corporate bonds is 10 percent, while Treasury bonds of similar maturity are yielding 8.5 percent. The company which issued the corporate bond decides to call the bonds. You are forced to sell them back to the company. Now, when interest rates are lower, you have cash to invest rather than a high-yield bond.

Not so with Treasury notes and bonds. These are not callable. If you had purchased the Treasury bonds yielding 11.5 percent, you would still be collecting the 11.5 percent. Thus, *when interest rates are high, and especially if you feel they may go down in the future, long-term Treasury bonds can be an excellent investment.* As a consequence of the call feature, corporate bonds clearly have more inherent market risk than Treasury notes or bonds.

Government-backed mortgage securities also may be attractive if you are seeking long-term investment of your funds. Two government-insured investments are "Fannie Maes," securities issued by the Federal National Mortgage Association (FNMA) and "Ginnie Maes," securities issued by the Government National Mortgage Association (GNMA). FNMA purchases mortgages from approved holders using the proceeds from various notes and bonds which it sells. Unlike FNMA, which is a publicly held corporation, GNMA is a government-owned corporation which also purchases mortgages using the proceeds from the securities which it sells.

When you purchase government-backed mortgage securities, you receive a flow-through of interest and principal payments as the mortgages are paid off. You might, for example, purchase into a pool of mortgages with an average maturity of 20 years. In this case you would expect to recover a portion of your investment each year, along with interest during the 20 years. Since little principal is repaid at the start of a mortgage and more toward the end, you could expect to recover your investment in the same way (little initially and more in following years). Similarly, you would anticipate receiving higher interest payments initially and lower interest payments as you recover more and more of your principal.

If many homeowners whose mortgages are in the pool should decide to move or refinance their mortgages, the securities may be paid off earlier than anticipated. *This frequently occurs if mortgage interest rates decrease and many people refinance.* If this should happen, you would recover your investment earlier than anticipated and be faced with lower-yielding investments in which to reinvest your money. *Furthermore, if interest rates should rise, the market value of the pool will decrease.* Thus, if you should need to sell your portion of the pool before the mortgages in the pool are repaid, you may incur a loss. Therefore, FNMA and GNMA investments, while government guaranteed, are certainly not without market risk.

Having to deal with reinvestment of principal, whether early or as scheduled, may pose a problem for some investors. Therefore, some mortgage-purchase investment plans provide for automatic reinvestment of your principal in new mortgages. Of course, when the funds are reinvested, they are reinvested at current interest rates which may be higher or lower than the average yield of the original portfolio of mortgages.

Government-guaranteed mortgages are more attractive to many investors than Treasury notes or bonds because they have a higher yield and there is little difference in risk of default. They are much less liquid, however, than Treasury notes or bonds, and, as noted earlier, if interest rates decrease, you may find many homeowners refinancing, so that you will be repaid earlier than anticipated. In fact, in periods of decreasing interest rates, if homeowners do refinance, you may find that the overall return on government-backed mortgage securities is actually less than on Treasury bonds, since you are forced to reinvest at lower rates. Also, if interest rates increase, and you want to sell your portion of the mortgage pool, you may incur a loss. Nonetheless, you may want to consider such securities for use in an IRA or to generate income at retirement to supplement your pension and Social Security.

CORPORATE SECURITIES

Corporations sell two primary types of securities which are available for investment: common stock and bonds. In addition, some companies sell preferred stock. *Common stock* represents a partial ownership of a company and therefore is called an "equity" investment. Common stockholders vote on major corporate issues and receive dividends if the company declares them. Dividends are fully taxable if paid from the company's earnings and profits and may increase or decrease depending upon the firm's profits from year to year. Stock and other corporate securities are sold through stock brokers. Furthermore, some commercial banks provide brokerage services.

Common stock is not risk-free with respect to default. Companies do go bankrupt, and stockholders may lose all of their investment. This, however, is unusual. The greater risk with common stock concerns the general level of stock prices, which are greatly affected by changes in interest rates. Therefore, *common stock exposes the owner to substantial market risk.*

As a practical matter, corporate shareholders exercise virtually no control over the company. So you have three options with common stock: buy, hold, or sell. The question, of course, is which stock to purchase.

Corporate Securities

Although many methods of analysis are being used, we have profited from the procedure outlined in Chapter 6. If you are interested in becoming directly involved with common stock trading, we suggest a thorough study of both the fundamental and technical procedures presented in Chapter 6.

Corporate bonds are a form of long-term corporate debt. Bonds frequently mature in ten to 20 years from the date of issue and pay interest semiannually. The interest is fully taxable. Most corporate bonds are sold in $1,000 denominations. Once issued, most corporate bonds are traded regularly on a securities exchange. Thus, if you want to sell prior to maturity, this can be accomplished easily. Similarly, if you want to purchase a bond which matures in a short period, this can also be accomplished.

Corporate bond yields are generally higher than Treasury bonds of comparable maturity, and even CDs having shorter maturities. The reason involves risk. Corporate bonds do entail some degree of risk of default; corporations have gone bankrupt and bondholders have lost their investments. Consequently, we recommend purchasing investment-grade bonds with a *minimum* rating of "BBB" by Standard and Poor's and "Baa" by Moody's. You can ascertain ratings easily by contacting your stockbroker or consulting these references in your public library. See Chapter Nine for details.

Another reason why corporate bonds are riskier than CDs is that the principal value of a CD remains constant while the principal value of a corporate bond varies daily. Corporate bonds therefore entail more market risk than CDs. This, of course, is the same with Treasury bonds and notes, as described earlier. Even though you pay a penalty for early withdrawal of a CD, you still recover your principal amount if you withdraw your money prior to maturity.

Not necessarily so with corporate or Treasury bonds. As interest rates fluctuate, the market prices of bonds increase or decrease. If you sell prior to maturity, you may suffer a loss on the sale. Of course, if you keep a corporate or Treasury bond to maturity, you will recover the $1,000 face value. As noted earlier, however, most (but not all) corporate bonds issued during periods of high interest are callable. However, many callable bonds may not be called prior to a date specified in the bond agreement. Your securities broker can tell you if and when a particular bond is callable.

If interest rates decrease, the bonds may be callable only after the date specified in the bond agreement. Therefore, by careful shopping, you may be able to purchase some high-yielding corporate bonds which are not callable for a few years. If the bonds are called, you then would recover your investment much earlier than anticipated and have to reinvest at lower interest rates. CDs and Treasury Bonds and Notes are not callable and therefore are less risky than corporate bonds.

Although listed under the heading of "Corporate Securities," *zero-coupon bonds* may be corporate, Treasury, or tax-exempt. Similarly, some banks offer zero-coupon CDs. Zero-coupon bonds differ from other bonds in that they do not pay semiannual interest; rather, they are sold at a price substantially less than their maturity value (normally $1,000). In this respect, they are similar to Series EE Bonds. The interest received is the difference between the purchase price and the maturity value. Unlike Series EE Bonds, however, the tax on the interest may not be deferred. Thus, you have to pay tax each year on interest which you don't actually receive. The interest is incorporated into the market price, which generally increases year by year until maturity is reached.

The negative tax consequences of zero-coupon bonds (having to pay income taxes on interest you don't receive) limit their attractiveness. Is there any attraction? *Treasury or high-quality corporate zero-coupon bonds are good for IRAs and similar tax-deferred accounts,* because the negative tax aspects are automatically eliminated. You might, for example, use your $2,000 IRA contribution to purchase four zero-coupon bonds at $500 each for a total of $2,000. If they mature in seven years, you would be sure of having $4,000 in your account at that time.

Zero-coupon bonds could prove to be a good investment since you will not have to worry about reinvesting either the principal amount or interest for seven years. This contrasts, for example, with the purchase of a three-year CD. After three years, you must decide how to reinvest the proceeds from the CD. Of course, a seven-year CD would also eliminate the reinvestment problem for seven years, but a seven-year CD normally would have a lower yield than a seven-year, zero-coupon corporate bond. As noted earlier, locking yourself into a seven-year zero coupon bond or CD exposes you to market risk. If interest rates should increase, you may not be able to take advantage of newly issued, higher-yielding investments.

In addition, with zero-coupon bonds, you don't have to be concerned with reinvestment of interest or dividends. For example, if you invested your IRA contribution in typical corporate or Treasury bonds, every six months you would have to deal with reinvesting the interest payments. Since the amount of those payments would be small, the investment options are limited, and you would likely be forced to invest the interest in a low-interest-rate account, an IRA variable-interest account, or some similar account. Since zero-coupon bonds offer advantages, there must be a cost. The cost is a lower interest rate than you would receive on a similar quality corporate or Treasury bond.

Some corporations also issue *preferred stock*. Preferred stock does not represent ownership in the company in the same sense that the common stockholders own a share of the company. In fact, *preferred stock is similar to corporate bonds,* except that most preferred stock is perpetual in nature. That is, it does not mature but many preferred issues do have call features, which, like those on corporate bonds, permit the issuing company to repurchase the preferred stock. Thus, preferred stock has some (but limited) risk of default and some market risk.

Unlike common stock, which may enjoy increases in dividends and market price if the firm's earnings increase, preferred stock dividends normally are fixed. If the yield (dividend divided by the market price) on a preferred stock is sufficiently high, then you might want to consider it as an alternative to corporate bonds.

Generally, however, the yield on preferred is less than corporate bonds. With a lower yield and the possibility for being called, why is preferred stock purchased? The reason involves a quirk in the tax law that excludes 80 percent of dividends received by a corporation from Federal income tax. So if a corporation had a substantial amount of funds which it wanted to park for a year or more, another corporation's preferred stock would provide a higher *after-tax* yield than nearly any interest-bearing investment.

Should you purchase preferred stock? Probably not, unless you own a business that is incorporated and you have money in the corporation you need to invest for some period of time.

MUTUAL FUNDS

Mutual funds represent a pooling of investor dollars to create a fund which is managed by professional portfolio managers. Mutual funds have become extremely popular in recent years for the following reasons:

- *They offer a way to purchase into a very diversified portfolio of securities with a relatively small investment*—sometimes as little as $250. With a diversified portfolio, risk of default is minimized.

They do, of course, have the same market risk as the securities that make up the fund's portfolio. If the value of the securities in the portfolio increases, the value of the mutual fund shares increases and vice versa.
- *They provide professional portfolio management,* which relieves you of the burden of selecting securities for your own portfolio.
- *They offer automatic reinvestment of dividends, interest, and other gains.* You are not faced with the question of how to invest a $50 dividend, for example.
- *They offer many different types of portfolios.* Some mutual funds purchase growth stocks, others income stocks, others bonds, tax-exempt securities, T-Bills, and so on. And you may be able to switch your investment among funds of various types managed by the same group—often by telephone.

But there are no free rides! Mutual funds have a cost. You usually must pay an entry fee (called a "load") of 2 to 7 percent or sometimes an exit fee. In addition, the portfolio managers charge for their services (usually around 2 percent per year) and sometimes perform very poorly.

Some mutual funds are "no-load" funds. That is, they do not charge an entry fee. Caution is noted, however. In recent years, some funds which advertise themselves as "no load" have been charging an additional annual fee called a "12(b) fee." This fee is a direct charge against investor equity. In addition to the management fee, this fee may be as high as 5 percent per year. Consequently, selecting a mutual fund requires careful study.

Generally, mutual funds are liquid. You can take out your money when you want. In some instances, however, you may not be able to recover your investment rapidly. If many owners of mutual fund shares want to redeem their shares at the same time, the mutual fund may not have the necessary cash on hand. Should this be the case, it will have to sell securities, which could take time. Therefore, you may not always be able to recover your investment quickly from a mutual fund.

Money magazine provides useful assistance in selecting one or more mutual funds that meet your needs. *Money* provides a "fund watch" indicating those funds with the best performance during recent periods and for several years. They also provide sales charges, minimum initial investment, and telephone numbers (toll free) for the better performing mutual funds. If past performance is an indicator of future performance, then this information can prove helpful. If you do want to become in-

Tax-Deferred Annuities

volved in the stock or bond markets, mutual funds may prove to be an easily accessible route.

MONEY MARKET MUTUAL FUNDS

Money market mutual funds, commonly called money market funds, are a particular type of mutual fund. Their portfolios consist of short-term U.S. Treasury, corporate, and other obligations. These funds are similar to the money-market deposit accounts offered by savings institutions. Since the names are so similar, they sometimes are confused. Although the primary purpose of both is the deposit of money for short periods of time, they differ in the following ways:

1. *Money market mutual funds are not insured by FDIC or FSLIC* and therefore may have a slightly greater risk of default than a saving institution's money-market deposit account. This risk essentially can be eliminated by investing in a money market mutual fund which limits its purchases to short-term U.S. Treasury obligations.

2. *Money market mutual funds usually pay a slightly higher rate of interest than money-market deposit accounts.*

3. *Check writing privileges are available for many money market mutual funds.* There may be a minimum dollar limit for check writing, such as $500. Also, there may be a limit on the number of checks you may write each month.

Since money-market mutual funds are similar to bank money-market deposit accounts, they serve the same basic function—a place to park your money for short periods of time. The money-market mutual fund may be particularly useful if you own shares in a mutual fund managed by the same investment group. Suppose, for example, you had money invested in a mutual fund consisting of common stock, and you believe that the stock market is likely to decline. You could switch your funds from the stock market mutual fund into the money-market mutual fund.

TAX-DEFERRED ANNUITIES

Tax-deferred, single-premium annuities are sold by many life insurance companies and some stock brokers in amounts ranging from $5,000 to

$250,000. The interest or other income generated in these accounts is tax deferred until the money is withdrawn from the account. If the purchaser should die, however, the beneficiary need not pay income tax on the accrued interest. Of course, the annuity is subject to inheritance tax.

Interest rates on these annuities are usually guaranteed for a period of one to three years. After that they vary from period to period. Returns are approximately equal to what you would receive on a CD. The benefit, of course, is tax-deferred interest. This makes annuities attractive for retirement savings, but, of course, not as a place to invest IRA or pension contributions, since the return on IRAs is already tax deferred.

LET'S SUM UP

You clearly have many choices for investing your money. Each has its own particular function in your overall portfolio. For example, a money market account or money market mutual fund would be a good place to place your "rainy day" account.

Savings for college could be kept in Series EE Savings Bonds or corporate bonds. Retirement savings in your IRA might be invested in bank CDs, mutual funds, corporate bonds, or corporate stock. Series EE bonds and deferred annuities offer other ways to save for retirement.

We recommend that you study Chapters 5, 6, and 7 before you make any investment decisions. Then you will be in a position to make investment decisions that meet your specific financial goals.

5

YOUR CORE INVESTMENTS

"When I was young I thought money was the most important thing in life. Now that I am old, I know it is."

oscar wilde

Now that you have an understanding of several investment options, you can plan your core investments. These are your most important investments—those that will form the basis of your financial independence.

This chapter looks at a number of basic financial planning matters:

- Saving money on your mortgage payments
- Planning for a secure retirement
- Providing funds for your children's educations
- Building an emergency fund
- Saving money on car payments

Having financial goals is a key to obtaining financial independence and an important element in establishing your core investments. We recommend that you establish the following five goals and use them as the basis for developing your core investments. Each is discussed in this chapter.

1. *Paying off your mortgage at least five years prior to your anticipated retirement.* We recommend planning to pay it off by age 55 *or earlier* if possible. You may not be considering retirement at age 55, but having your mortgage paid off at that time will provide you with *added financial flexibility and increase your planning options.*
2. *Plan for your retirement.* Many people don't plan for retirement until they are 50 or older. In many instances this is too late. Both you and your spouse should start to plan for retirement now.
3. *Plan to fund your children's college education.* College can be a big expense. You must plan early and save systematically if you expect to provide your children with college educations which do not disrupt your standard of living.
4. *Continue to build the "rainy day" account we discussed in Chapter One.* Your emergency funds could be depleted rapidly if you encountered a medical emergency not covered by insur-

ance, faced a layoff, wanted to change careers, or needed to perform unexpected home repairs.
5. *Try to set aside money for replacement of such items as furniture and applicances.* Nothing lasts forever, except automobile and installment loan payments! Regular saving for major purchases will save you thousands of dollars in interest charges.

DIVERSITY AND LIQUIDITY: A STARTING POINT

As you start to build your core investment program, you must have both diversity and liquidity in your assets and accounts. Your "rainy day account" may start you in both directions. It should contain about three months of take-home salary for both you and your spouse and be deposited in an easily accessible money market fund or similar account. This money is liquid. Hopefully, you will be able to add to it as you enjoy salary increases, and *it will form the basis of your liquidity.*

If your "rainy day accounts" (you will need two if both you and your spouse work) are in money market or other very liquid investments, you have already started to diversify. Your largest investment at this point probably is your home. Although a home may not be a liquid investment, you may be able to secure a *home equity loan* by using your home as collateral. This can increase the liquidity of your home investment, but at a price. Home equity loans often carry high interest rates and take some time to secure. Your "rainy day accounts," by contrast, are very liquid. The money in these accounts is available immediately, if needed. If both you and your spouse have "rainy day accounts," consider keeping them in separate financial institutions. This increases your diversification while maintaining your liquidity.

As you undertake your core investment program, be sure to retain sufficient liquidity and diversification. Don't, for example, become obsessed with any one goal, such as paying off your mortgage or saving for a new car. Maintain balance in all of your financial affairs.

Consistency is the Rule

The most important factor in your goal of attaining financial independence is consistency in your financial program. This may mean paying a little extra on your mortgage every month, regularly funding your pension or savings account for retirement, or placing a small amount in your contingency fund each month. How you choose to invest your savings depends upon your personal financial goals and your interest in various possible investments. Whatever investment vehicle you choose, invest consistently and diversify.

As noted in Chapter 1, you need to set financial goals. You and your spouse need to agree on those goals and budget to meet them. Don't expect to become rich quickly. Yes, you could invest $2.00 per week in the lottery and become a millionaire, but the chances are extremely small that you will win. So forget the lottery, and save regularly!

A CLOSE LOOK AT YOUR MORTGAGE

"One of life's greatest pleasures: paying the last installment."

Chapter 2 told you how much you can save by paying off your mortgage early. Eliminating thousands of dollars of interest payments is only one edge of the two-edged financial sword of prepaying your mortgage. Consider the following example.

You purchase a home and have a $50,000, 10 percent, 30-year, fixed-rate mortgage. The payments are $438.79 per month. You decide to pay an additional $43.72 per month (total payment of $482.51 per month), which will reduce the payment period from 30 years to 20 years. Instead of paying $157,964.40 in interest and principal over 30 years, you pay $115,802.40 over 20 years, for a savings of $42,162 in interest! That large savings in interest payments is the first edge of the early prepayment sword.

With the mortgage eliminated, consider what you can accomplish if you continue to save an amount equal to the monthly payment you were making. If you save $482.51 per month for the next ten years and obtain only an 8 percent return, you will have amassed $88,272.77. If you obtained a higher rate of return—perhaps 10 percent—you would have almost $100,000, not to mention a mortgage-free home. Clearly, you can amass a very substantial amount of money simply by paying only an extra $43.72 per month, in this example, over the original 30-year mortgage period. This is the second edge of the early payment sword.

Take a moment to recap. If you pay $438.79 per month for 30 years, you will have paid off your mortgage. If you pay an additional $43.72 per month, you not only will pay off your mortgage, but you also likely will have accumulated another $100,000 as well. As noted in

Chapter 1, *compound interest can work magic for your financial future.*

Unless the interest rate on your mortgage is less than the rate you obtain on a low-risk investment, such as a Certificate of Deposit, we encourage you to pay a little extra each month. For example, if the interest rate on your mortgage is a low 8 percent, and you can obtain 10 percent on CDs, then you would be better advised to purchase the CDs. Even if the interest rate on your mortgage is low, you may still want to consider paying a little extra each month. You may find it far more difficult to accumulate the cash to buy a CD, for example, than put a little extra away each month for your mortgage.

As your income increases, you may want to increase your mortgage payment even more. Of course, you want to establish your "rainy day account" and also pay off all your charge accounts and any other high-interest loans before prepaying your mortgage.

PLANNING FOR A FINANCIALLY SECURE RETIREMENT

Most large companies and nearly all government agencies provide retirement plans for their employees. Many smaller companies do not have retirement plans. Those that do often provide adequate benefits only for the owners and highly paid managers.

Before you start to plan for your retirement you need to understand your employer's retirement benefit plan. That may sound unnecessary, but our experience has been that most people—even highly paid executives—do not know what their employer-provided retirement benefits will be. Many workers believe that because they are covered by pension plans, they don't have to give the matter any thought. This is just not so. *Pension plans vary greatly among employers. Benefits vary greatly depending on your salary, length of service, and age at retirement.* You need to take the time to review your pension benefits with your personnel officer. Once you understand what your benefits will be and when you will be eligible to start collecting them, you can start to plan for your retirement.

At this point, you need to understand some basic information about pension plans and your retirement needs. You will find this most helpful when you talk with your personnel officer.

1. *Assuming that your home is mortgage-free when you retire, you*

Planning for a Financially Secure Retirement

likely will need about 80 percent of your total pre-retirement, after-tax income to live comfortably. In addition, your income will have to be increased to compensate for inflation in order for you to maintain that standard of living. Your retirement income can come from five possible sources:

- Tax Qualified Retirement Plans (i.e., retirement plans approved by the Internal Revenue Service; for most people this would be the retirement plan provided by the employer)
- Social Security
- Individual Retirement Accounts (IRAs)
- Other investments
- Post-retirement employment

2. *Inflation will be around when you retire.* In dealing with increases in the cost of living, three basic types of plans need to be considered. You should know which one you are in. Here's a brief description:

- *One type of pension plan provides for fixed monthly payments, including Social Security.* During times of inflation, when Social Security benefits are increased, the pension portion of your monthly payment is reduced. This means your monthly payment remains constant. As time goes on, the pension portion of the payment will decrease, and you ultimately may receive only Social Security benefits. This is one of the worst, but most common plans.
- *Other pension plans provide for a fixed monthly payment in addition to your Social Security benefit.* Thus, in times of inflation, you will receive increases in your income resulting from increased Social Security benefits, but your pension benefits will remain constant. This type of pension plan (which does not provide for cost-of-living increases) is also very common. Some plans of this type provide you with an option to receive lower initial payments when you retire and increased payments in later years. You should consider this option when you approach retirement age if you are covered by this type of pension.
- The most generous retirement plans, such as those provided to some Federal government employees (including members of Congress) provide for regular monthly payments with cost-of-living increases. In addition, if the recipient is covered by Social Se-

curity, he or she also receives these payments. Other Federal plans are less generous than this plan and provide partial cost-of-living increases.

3. *You need to know the type of plan you are in and the benefits you are likely to receive.* You also need to know the Social Security benefits you likely will receive. When you seek this information, the dollar amount of the benefits is not nearly as critical as the *percentage of your pre-retirement income* you can expect to receive.

For example, suppose your personnel officer says you probably will receive a $20,000 pension and $8,000 in Social Security benefits at age 62. Unless you are close to age 62, this information has little value to you. In ten or 15 years, inflation could halve the purchasing power of benefits expressed in today's dollars. By contrast, if your personnel officer tells you that your pension probably will provide you with an amount equal to 40 percent of your take-home pay during the year prior to your retirement—and Social Security probably will provide another 20 percent—then you can start to plan.

4. *Some retirement plans permit additional employee contributions.* Some retirement plans permit employees to make contributions in excess of any required contribution (if a contribution indeed is required). By making regular contributions to your retirement plan, your retirement benefits will increase—possibly quite dramatically.

Check with your personnel officer and ask if you may make additional contributions. If you are permitted to do so, ask how much you may contribute and what effect the contributions will have on your retirement benefits. Again, the dollar amount of the increase in benefits is less important than the percentage increase in your benefits.

If, for example, an extra contribution of $50 per month to your pension fund would increase the percentage of take-home retirement income from 40 to 50 percent of your pre-retirement income, the extra contribution might be worthwhile.

5. *Since retirement plans vary so much, you should take time to become fully informed about a company's plan before accepting employment.* This is especially important if you are over 40 years of age.

6. *Changing jobs can have a severe effect on your pension.* Normally, if you are in a pension plan and leave after ten years (sometimes less) of service, you will have vested your benefits. This means that your employer's contribution and any contributions you have made will remain in the pension plan, and you will receive some pension when you retire.

Planning for a Financially Secure Retirement

The pension is likely to be small, and you may have to wait until age 62 or 65 to start receiving it. So before you consider switching jobs, inquire about vesting and the amount of future retirement benefits you are likely to receive.

If you change positions and have less than the number of years required to vest your pension, you may not be able to vest any of your benefits. Normally, this means that the employer will recover the contributions it made to your pension plan, and you will receive any contributions you may have made, along with interest. The interest rate frequently is very low, so you shouldn't expect to receive very much.

Our experience has been that it almost always is in your best interest to vest your pension when leaving employment. If you have worked, for example, with a company eight years and are considering a move, you might want to wait two more years, if the vesting period is ten years. The period required for vesting will be changing as a result of the Tax Reform Act of 1986. Be sure to check the vesting period with your personnel officer when considering a possible change in employment.

7. *Length of service means a great deal.* Many companies offer early retirement programs—possibly at age 55 to employees with 25 or more years of employment. If you started working at such a company at age 30, you could be eligible for early retirement at age 55. If you started at age 40, you obviously would be ineligible.

In addition, length of service may affect your benefits in two ways. First, working for one company 40 years may bring you a significantly *greater total pension* than working ten years for four different companies, even if you vested after each ten-year period. *Changing employers can greatly reduce your pension benefits.*

The second factor involving length of service concerns the weight each year of service has in the formula used to determine your benefits. Some plans "weigh" each year of service equally. For example, some pension plans pay a percentage of the average of your last three years of salary. The percentage depends on the number of years worked. With 20 years of service, you might receive one-third of the average of your last three years of pay. With 30 years, you might receive one-half. With 40 years of service, you might receive two-thirds, and so forth. Each year of service has the same "weight." There are variations on the plans which "weigh" each year of service equally. For example, some plans compute benefits based on the average pay of your three highest pay years taken from your last five years of service.

Other plans do not weigh each year of service equally when determining your benefits. Such plans use a formula to determine your benefits. The formula may place very little weight on the first few years of service and very heavy weight on service over ten or 20 years.

8. *Many part-time employees are not covered by pension plans.* If you or your spouse is working part time, you should give careful consideration to working full time with a company that offers a pension plan—even if the hourly rate for the full-time position is lower. The long-term benefits of having a pension plan may far outweigh the difference in pay.

HOW TO INCREASE YOUR RETIREMENT INCOME

"The trouble with advice is that you seldom know whether it is good or bad until you no longer need it."

You can take several important actions to increase your retirement income:

1. *Increase your contribution to your pension, if this is permitted.*

2. *Change from part-time to full-time employment with pension coverage.* Not only will this increase pension benefits, but it also may increase your Social Security benefits as well.

3. *Open an individual retirement account (IRA) and contribute the maximum amount allowable by law.* This, of course, requires money. Some of our clients have found that when one spouse was working full-time and the other part-time, neither could afford to contribute. When the second spouse commenced working full-time, enough additional income was available to fully fund both their IRAs. Starting in 1987, for certain high-income taxpayers, the IRA contribution, although permitted, may not be fully tax deductible. See the following section for details.

4. *Consider obtaining additional job skills needed to secure higher paying employment.* This is especially important for a person who has been out of the workforce or has been working only part-time for a number of years. Education to obtain needed career skills can be the best investment you can make for the present and for the future. And, if your employer will pay for it, the cost to you will be minimal.

5. If you believe that your IRA will not be sufficient to meet your needs, *begin a regular savings program for retirement.*

6. If you are approaching retirement age, *determine if you may stay at your current position for a long period* (perhaps an extra two or three years), and what effect the additional service will have on your total

retirement package (pension, Social Security, IRA, or other savings). Also look into the possibility of part-time or full-time employment with another employer after retirement. You might also consider part-time employment with your present employer, if this is permitted.

7. *Consider moving into a smaller home.* Perhaps you can purchase a smaller home now and rent it for a few years while you prepare to live in it. Then, when you retire, sell your larger, more expensive home, pay off the mortgage on the smaller home, and invest the difference to add to your retirement income. As noted earlier, the first $125,000 in capital gains resulting from the sale of your home are generally not subject to federal tax.

Many excellent books have been written about retirement planning. A partial listing is included in Chapter 9. Since so many people already have IRAs, and many others will be opening them, IRAs are discussed in the following section.

INDIVIDUAL RETIREMENT ACCOUNTS

"The hardest thing in the world to understand is the income tax."
Albert Einstein

Even though recent tax legislation has reduced the number of people who may deduct IRA contributions from their taxable income, this topic is still very important for the following reasons:

- You may start an IRA or continue to make IRA contributions even if you are not permitted to deduct your contributions from your taxable income.
- You already may have one or more IRAs and want to know how to invest in the best possible way.

Individual Retirement Accounts offer a way to plan for retirement and for some may reduce current Federal income tax. Since January 1, 1982, IRAs have been available to all workers—including those who are self-employed and those who may already be covered by pension plans. Beginning in 1987, the tax deductibility of your IRA contributions may be limited, depending on your income and pension coverage. You will be eligible for an IRA tax deduction if:

1. You are not covered by an employer pension plan, or
2. You are covered by an employer pension plan but you have an

adjusted gross income below $40,000 if you file a joint return and below $25,000 if you file an individual return.

You will be eligible for a partial IRA deduction if you have an adjusted gross income between $40,000 and $50,000 on a joint return and between $25,000 and $35,000 on an individual return. Regardless of the tax deductibility of contributions, the taxes on the earnings from IRA accounts are tax deferred until you begin withdrawing funds.

You may place up to $2,000 per year into an IRA each year, or $2,250 if your spouse is not employed. If both are eligible and employed, then the maximum annual contribution is $4,000.

Contributing regularly to an IRA is the best way many people can plan for their senior years. IRAs offer:

- A means to *plan for retirement*
- A way to *defer taxes* to future years
- A way to become more *financially secure* and less dependent on Social Security and pension benefits

The tax on all of the income earned by your IRA contributions is *deferred* until the start of withdrawals. This means that it is not necessary to pay tax on the income generated from the contributions *now*—but that taxes will have to be paid on the money *as it is withdrawn from the IRA*. With one exception, all withdrawals from IRAs are subject to tax as *ordinary income*. Any contributions using *after-tax* income, beginning in 1987, will not be subject to tax when withdrawn.

Most people probably will be in lower tax brackets when they retire as a result of having *less income* and an *increased standard deduction* at age 65 or beyond. In any event, *the tax is postponed*. This is equivalent to getting an *interest-free loan* from Uncle Sam—a great deal!

IRAs are designed to provide for retirement income. Withdrawals may start at age $59\frac{1}{2}$ and *must* start by age $70\frac{1}{2}$. If you continue to work, contributions may be made until age $70\frac{1}{2}$. The laws covering IRAs allow a lot of *flexibility in retirement planning*.

For example, suppose you retired at age 62 and had enough income from a pension, other savings, and Social Security to cover living expenses. The money could remain in your IRA, continuing to earn tax-deferred returns, until mandatory withdrawals started at age $70\frac{1}{2}$. Or,

Individual Retirement Accounts

suppose you got a part-time job after retiring. If eligible, you still could continue to make contributions to an IRA.

Premature withdrawals are withdrawals made before age $59\frac{1}{2}$. Such withdrawals may be made *without penalty* if you are disabled. In such instances, the money withdrawn will be *taxed as ordinary income* (except any contributions using after-tax dollars). Since you would not be working, the actual tax paid on such withdrawals could be low.

If you make a premature withdrawal and are *not* ill or injured, the amount withdrawn will be subject to a "severe" penalty (excise tax) of 10 percent. For example, suppose you withdrew $1,000 before reaching age $59\frac{1}{2}$. A 10 percent tax would have to paid on the $1,000. *In addition,* the entire $1,000 also would be *taxed as ordinary income,* except any contributions using after-tax dollars. You also may be faced with premature withdrawal penalties for certain kinds of investments and for certain time periods. For example, if IRA funds were invested in certificates of deposit, and the certificates were redeemed prior to maturity, a premature withdrawal penalty would be assessed by the savings institution.

Consider another situation. Suppose you were unemployed for a period of time and needed to withdraw money from your IRA to meet your living expenses. The 10 percent penalty would have to be paid, and the withdrawals would be taxed as ordinary income. But, if you did not have other taxable income, the amount of tax liability in excess of the 10 percent penalty probably would be very little. So, *an IRA should be viewed as money for retirement and, if necessary, money for a major personal or financial problem.*

The timing of contributions to an IRA can be an important factor in determining retirement benefits. In general, contributions for a particular year may be made from January 1 of that year until the date a person files his or her Federal income tax for that year (usually on or before April 15 of the following year).

If funds are available, try to make your contribution to an IRA *early in January.* Waiting until income tax filing time the following year will reduce the earnings on your contributions.

Since IRAs may prove to be a very important source of income for your retirement, try to obtain the highest rate of return on contributions. Most people do not realize how much difference the rate of return will make on IRA retirement benefits. Recall Table 1-2 in Chapter 1 which shows how much you will accumulate at different rates of return.

Some investments will yield higher returns than others. Consequently, it pays to shop around. Keep these factors in mind:

1. *Risk:* Is it possible to lose any of your IRA savings? If so, what is the risk?
2. *Safety:* Is there any insurance covering the IRA funds, in case the institution where the funds are invested should have financial problems?
3. *Time:* How much of your time will be involved in managing your IRA investment?
4. *Return:* How much return is it possible to get, consistent with the limits on risk exposure, the desired safety, and the limits on time you have available to manage your IRA investment?

Return is important—the higher the return, the higher the retirement income. However, the money saved for retirement should be invested prudently so that your savings are not lost.

Where to Put Your IRA Money

The choice of investment options is staggering and growing. When your IRA has grown to $10,000 or more, many hands will be eagerly waiting to help you invest (and perhaps lose) your money. In order of *decreasing risk,* here are some investment alternatives for your IRA:

- *Self-directed:* You set up an account with a stock broker and trade securities. This is risky and requires a lot of time for prudent management.
- *Mutual Funds:* The more aggressive funds are usually riskier.
- *Money Market Accounts.*
- *Fixed-rate certificates* (CDs).

Since diversification tends to reduce risk, we recommend you consider placing IRAs in government-insured, fixed-rate bank or savings and loan certificates of deposit. Some institutions offer higher interest rates for IRA accounts than on ordinary CDs. It pays to shop around, since large city banks and savings and loan institutions frequently will pay as much as a percent or more higher interest for the same maturity IRA certificates than local institutions.

PLANNING FOR COLLEGE EDUCATION

"Education is the greatest gift of all if you can afford it."

Going to college can be very expensive. Planning ahead for college education can take a lot of the sting out of the potentially high cost. Some colleges offer unique financing plans—a trend that will likely continue.

One university will accept $4,450 as total payment for four years' tuition when the child is born. The "catch," of course, is that the child may not choose to attend that school or may not meet admissions' standards. Other universities are providing similar plans. "Creative financing" plans are great if you have the money when your child is born and you are sure that he or she will want to attend college. Although you may not be able or want to pay now for college tuition in 18 years, other colleges do offer financing plans which may be helpful. For example:

- The University of Pennsylvania offers a comprehensive financing plan with ten years to repay.
- Fairleigh Dickinson University offers a plan whereby if one of your children attends, a second may attend paying half tuition.

These plans may sound "gimmicky," but they are on the increase as colleges seek to assist parents in paying rising tuition costs. We recommend that you try to save for your children's education, taking advantage of the magic of compound interest described in Chapter 1 in conjunction with Series EE Savings Bonds and the Uniform Gift to Minor Accounts discussed in the next section.

The best time to start preparing for your child's college education is at birth. Friends and relatives typically want to know what they can give the newborn child. We suggest you tell them you are going to start a college fund and would appreciate contributions toward it. The amount you will have in 18 years depends on what you are able to place in this account and the rate of return obtained. Table 5-1 gives some possibilities.

The accumulated savings shown here will go a long way toward covering college costs at many good-quality institutions. But costs are increasing, and you should plan to add to your child's college fund each year. Here are two practical suggestions:

1. *Ask grandparents to contribute on the child's birthday.* If another $200 were contributed each year, beginning with the first

TABLE 5-1 College Fund Accumulations in 18 Years

	Amount Initially in Fund			
	$1,000	$2,000	$3,000	$4,000
Accumulation at Rate of				
8%	$3,996	$7,992	$11,988	$15,984
10	5,560	11,120	16,680	22,240
12	7,690	15,380	23,070	30,760

birthday, another $6,750 would accumulate at 8 percent interest. At 10 percent, the account would grow by $8,109.
2. *Add a small amount each month.* If you added $20 per month, the accumulation would grow by an additional $9,601 at 8 percent interest. If the account were to grow at 10 percent, your $20 per month would add another $12,011.

College costs are going up so we can't guarantee that you will accumulate enough to permit your child to attend the most expensive institutions. But you certainly will be off to a good start if you save systematically.

UNIFORM GIFT TO MINORS ACCOUNT

For each child, you should consider establishing a *Uniform Gift to Minors Account*. This could be established with a reputable brokerage firm in or near your community or a bank trust department. Have yourself listed as both donor and custodian of the account. You will have to obtain a Social Security number for your child. Call your regional Social Security office to find out how to do this.

Income earned in the account is taxable but may only be taxable as income to your child. Note, however, that under provisions of the Tax Reform Act of 1986, a child's net unearned income in excess of $1,000 may be taxed at the parents' marginal tax rate if the child is under 14 years of age. However, if the child has earned income, a portion of the $1,000 of unearned income also may be taxed at the parent's marginal tax rate.

Under the law, money donated to a Uniform Gift to Minors Account is considered an irrevocable gift. As custodian, however, you have the right to use the funds in the account in a way that benefits the minor. Using the assets in the account for tuition, books, and room and board during the child's college years more than meets all the standards set forth for such an account. When your minor child attains his or her majority, any residual funds in the account are reregistered in your child's name, and your custodianship is terminated. Of course, at that time, your child gains control of the account and may spend the funds as he or she sees fit.

We recommend that you invest funds in this account in one of three ways:

1. If your child is very young, consider a growth common-stock mutual fund. Historically, stocks have outperformed bonds and CDs. When your child is approaching college age (between ages 15 and 18), and if the stock market is doing well, convert the common-stock mutual fund to a money-market mutual fund, a bond mutual fund, or CDs. As noted in Chapter 4, you may be able to switch from a common-stock growth fund to a bond or money-market mutual fund without cost as long as the funds are managed by the same group.

2. If you do not want to risk investment in a common-stock mutual fund, consider a bond mutual fund or purchase high-grade corporate bonds that mature in four to seven years and will not be called prior to maturity. If you have limited funds in the account, purchasing shares of a bond mutual fund may be preferable, since the brokerage fees to purchase one or two bonds is high.

3. If your child is approaching college age, consider CDs with maturities sequenced to meet college costs.

We believe that the saving strategy outlined here will reduce the strain on your family's budget when your children reach college age. To keep funding on target, you may want to share information with interested relatives, perhaps providing them with periodic reports. Also, let your children know about the account.

A CONTINGENCY ACCOUNT

No matter how well you plan, you will have periodic financial crises. They cannot be avoided. Also, you may periodically find investment opportunities that you may want to take advantage of immediately. We therefore recommend establishing and building a contingency fund in addition to your "rainy day account" described in Chapter 1.

Determining how much you need in your contingency account depends on several factors:

- *Your home mortgage:* The more equity you have in your home, the less you need in your contingency account.
- *Life insurance:* The larger your contingency account, the less life insurance you need.
- *Your need for liquidity:* The less liquid your other assets, the more you need in your contingency account.
- *Your age and your spouse's age:* The older you are, the more you need in your contingency account.
- *Your job stability:* The more stable your job, the less you need in your contingency account.
- *Your children:* The younger your children, the more you need in your contingency account. We advise that you try to build a contingency fund of at least $10,000 by the time you are 40 years old. This may be easier said than done, especially if you are putting a little extra into your monthly mortgage payment, funding an IRA, and saving for your children's educations. To help you start, why not put $30 per month into your contingency account? If you start at age 23, you will have $12,954 at age 40 (17 years), figuring an 8 percent return. If you can save only $20 per month, you will accumulate $8,637 by age 40. Of course, if you obtain a higher rate of return, your accumulation will grow even faster.

THOSE AWFUL CAR PAYMENTS

Two people were discussing automobiles. "Yes, sir," said one. "I believe the best economy is to trade every two years. That's what I've done, and do you know what?" he continued proudly, "I haven't missed a payment in 14 years."

Almost everyone needs an automobile. Unfortunately, cars are very expensive. In fact, the average driver spends over $3,000 per year to own and operate a car. Can you reduce the costs? Yes! Keep your car for longer periods, and save as much as you can to put down on a new car (maybe you can buy it outright).

Consider the following example. You want to purchase a $12,000 car and have $2,000 for a down payment. You finance $10,000 at 13 percent over 48 months. The monthly payment is $268.28 for a total of $12,877. You paid $2,877 in interest. And the tax deductibility of the interest deduction is being phased out!

Your "new" car is now four years old, and you are thinking about purchasing a new one for $14,000. The price increase resulted from inflation. Your car is worth $4,000 in trade. You could go through the same cycle and continue to pay $268.28 per month for another four years. Don't do it.

Keep your car. Plan to spend an extra $40 per month ($480 per year) for maintenance, and save the remaining $228.28. In three years, you will accumulate $9,252, based on an 8 percent return. Out of this amount, you earned $1,035 in interest.

Your car is now seven years old and possibly worth $3,000 as a trade in on a $15,000 new car. You will be short by $2,747 ($15,000 − $3,000 − $9,252 = $2,747). Finance the $2,747 for one year. Assuming a 13 percent interest rate, your payments will be $245.36 per month. At the end of the year, you own your car. Start saving again. If you save $245.36 per month for 36 months at 8 percent, you will accumulate $9,946, of which $1,113 is interest you received. The $9,946, plus your four-year-old car, likely will buy you a new car—and you won't have any car payments.

Now, if you save just $200 per month, you should be able to purchase a new car every four years with no car payments. At 8 percent, $200 per month will grow to $11,270 in four years, of which $1,670 is interest you received. The $11,270, plus your four-year-old car, should buy you a new one.

By using this simple plan, you can save about $70 in car payments each month. Recall that your original payment was $268.28, and now you are saving $200 per month—for a difference of $68.28 per month. Collecting interest is much better than paying interest. Of course, the same strategy can be applied to saving for replacement furniture, major appliances, and other "big ticket" items.

Perhaps the saying is true, *"The difference between a rich person and a poor person is that the rich person collects interest while the poor person pays interest"*.

Leasing an Automobile

With the price of automobiles constantly increasing, many automobile dealers and leasing companies have advertised leasing in an attempt to increase sales. Many advertisements appear very attractive. For example, most lessors require only a small security deposit and the first month's lease payment (rent) to enable you to drive out in a new car. If you already own a car that you plan to trade in, you may:

1. Dispose of it yourself and pocket the money.
2. Turn it over to the lessor and apply its value against the lease, which will result in lower monthly rental payments. Many lessors will take trade-ins, especially those associated directly with new car dealers.
3. Turn it over to the lessor, apply part of its value to cover the security deposit and first month's rental, and pocket the remainder.

Thus, instead of trading in your car to purchase a new one, and perhaps adding a few thousand dollars to reduce the monthly car payments, you literally can "tap the equity" in your present car by selling it to the lessor. You drive away in a new car and have money in your pocket.

This sounds very attractive, but there are "no free lunches." What are the disadvantages? There are two:

1. You don't own the car at the end of the lease period, which is usually 36, 48, or 60 months. If you purchased the car, you would own it when it comes time to throw away the payment book. You may purchase the car at the end of the lease, but this likely will result in your having to finance it with new payments—and no new car.
2. Most automobile leases limit mileage to an average of 12,000 to 15,000 per year over the life of the lease. If you drive more than the allowable mileage limit, you must pay a substantial "excess mileage penalty" at the end of the lease. This may be $.05 to $.25 per mile. Suppose, for example, you leased for 36 months and had 36,000 allowable miles, but you actually drove 46,000 miles. If the penalty were $.10 per mile, you would owe the lessor $1,000!

Although leasing may appear to be very attractive at the start of the lease, the cost over the long term is likely to exceed the cost of ownership.

If you are considering leasing, send $.50 for *A Consumer's Guide to Vehicle Leasing* to the Federal Trade Commission, Department 458P, Consumer Information Center, Pueblo, CO 81009.

LET'S SUM UP

By setting aside just a small amount each month, you can:

- Increase your retirement benefits
- Save thousands of dollars in interest by paying off your mortgage early
- Fund your children's educations
- Build a contingency fund
- Save thousands of dollars in automobile, appliance, and furniture financing charges

Establish your financial program and stick to it!

In the following two chapters, we examine investment strategies that can provide you with above-average returns on your discretionary funds. You likely will find your fortune growing rapidly if you follow our guidelines. So keep moving ahead to achieve your financial goals while becoming your own best financial advisor.

6

THE DEVIL AND DOW JONES

"Take time to deliberate, but when time for action arrives, stop thinking and go on."

andrew jackson

Chapter 4 provides you with a comprehensive analysis of various kinds of financial investments, ranging from passbook savings accounts to corporate stock. We also noted how particular investments could meet your individual needs. For example, Series EE Savings Bonds have the advantage of being risk-free with respect to default and also permit you to defer income tax on the interest for a period of years. In addition, you can purchase them by means of payroll deduction at your place of work. Each kind of financial investment has particular characteristics that meet the needs of certain groups of investors. This chapter should help you gain an understanding of these financial matters:

- The advantages of owning corporate securities
- Building a diversified portfolio
- Learning the basics of analyzing stocks
- Understanding the basics of fundamental and technical stock analysis
- Understanding the basics of selling options and the potential profit you can make from their sale
- Obtaining a high, tax-free return on municipal bonds.

INVESTING IN SECURTIES

Our goal in this chapter is not to recommend that you invest in corporate common stock or other financial securities. Antiques, coins, stamps, real estate, or other collectibles may best meet your needs and interests. Many people, however, do invest in stock and other financial securities either directly or indirectly through mutual funds. Here are some reasons why:

1. *Unlike the markets for collectibles and real estate, the markets for securities are well organized.* You can determine the current market value of most financial securities simply by looking in the business section of your newspaper.

2. *The mechanisms for trading securities are relatively simple from*

the investor's standpoint. Orders may be placed simply and quickly over the telephone.

3. *A wealth of information is readily available on nearly all financial securities.* See Chapter 9 for a listing of books on securities and for details on using your public library to obtain investment information.

4. *Unlike collectibles, storage and deterioration present no problems with securities.* This is not to say that the values of securities will not decrease, but you don't need an attic, basement, or garage to store securities. Several years ago one of the authors purchased 50,000 newly minted pennies and stored them in plastic containers in his attic. After two years, he inspected the pennies only to find that some were corroded, despite the plastic containers. He finally sold the lot for face value!

5. Purchasing securities does not require dealing with renters (as is the case with real estate), and you don't have to travel miles to search through a musty basement in hope of finding some overlooked antique. *Purchasing securities does require a lot of time and study, however. It is not a simple matter, and many small investors regularly lose money in securities.*

6. *Investing in securities offers tremendous opportunities for diversification.* Basically, diversification can be attained in two ways: by purchasing various kinds of securities (some U.S. Savings Bonds, some Certificates of Deposit, some stocks, etc.) and by investing in several institutions or companies. If, for example, you have more than $10,000 in CDs, you would want to consider purchasing them from more than one savings institution. Similarly, if you purchase stocks, you want to own the stock of companies representing various industries.

7. *Investing in securities offers a way to provide the liquidity you will need.* By liquidity, we mean how easy it is to convert a security into cash. A checking account, for example, is very liquid. You merely go to your bank and cash a check. By contrast, stock is generally less liquid, since most trades have a five-working-day settlement (the time until you receive payment is five days). Real estate and collectibles are very illiquid; it can take months to sell a property at a reasonable price.

As noted in Chapter 1, you should maintain at least three months' take-home salary in your "rainy day account." This money should be very liquid—perhaps held in a money-market account. As you become more financially independent, you will want to achieve a balance between liquid assets and those which are less liquid. Securities are a good way to accomplish this goal.

Securities as Discretionary Investments

"The higher you climb the mountain, the harder the wind blows."
Sam Cummings

The investment procedures described in this chapter are to be used once you have your core investment plan organized and funded. We would not suggest that you even consider taking funds earmarked for buying a house and use them in the hope of making a quick return in the stock market. By the same token, money you've set aside for your children's educations would be better placed in such conservative investments as bank CDs or bonds rather than in stock purchases. *We also would not advocate that you purchase stock for your IRA account, unless you have a very solid pension plan in addition to the IRA.*

To us, discretionary money is money you literally can afford to lose without feeling any change in your standard of living—either now or in the future. If you can invest your funds and obtain an average rate of return of 6 to 10 percent a year over the rate of inflation, consider yourself fortunate. You may be able to accomplish this if you are willing to read and study financial reports and the wealth of other information on the financial markets. *You can and will lose money some of the time. You must pull for the long run and learn from your mistakes.* Achieving a solid financial position takes years, not months. Finally, you must never become discouraged and place your securities in a drawer and forget them. You might open it one day and find a gold mine, but you are just as likely to find wallpaper!

THE STOCK MARKET—A PERSPECTIVE

Few institutions, except perhaps the fun house at the amusement park, attract and scare more people than the stock market. The specter of Wall Street, with millions of dollars being made and lost every day, fascinates many of us. Remember Uncle Bill who invested $1,000 in Xerox back in 1960 and is now rich? But then there's old Mr. Jones down the street who saw the value of his stocks decrease dramatically during the mid-1970s.

Yes, the stock market is risky, but the risks can be evaluated to some degree. And it is this fact that opens the door to the *prudent* use of securities in your overall financial planning.

Let's be clear about the term *risk*. The lottery is extraordinarily risky. Your chances of winning anything, let alone the big million-plus jackpots, are virtually nil. That's a simple and absolutely consistent mathematical fact. But your risk is limited to the amount you spend on the lottery tickets. You probably will be throwing that money away, and most people realize this. Why, then, do people buy lottery tickets? Simply because lottery tickets are inexpensive and offer a possibility of "getting rich quick."

Ownership of rental real estate, on the other hand, entails a different kind of risk from that involved in playing the lottery. In real estate, you obviously have much more invested than the price of a lottery ticket. Unlike the lottery, however, *you have some control over the "game" in real estate.* If you are a good manager, you can make a profit in real estate. But if you are a poor manager or have not taken the time to investigate thoroughly the properties you are considering for purchase, you can lose a lot more than the price of a lottery ticket!

By contrast, a passbook savings account, with principal insured by the Federal Deposit Insurance Corporation, entails much less risk than either the lottery or rental real estate. Of course, the "tradeoff" is the low rate of growth—perhaps only a few percent a year—in a passbook savings account.

These examples demonstrate one critical element needed to assess the degree of risk in any investment—knowledge of the investment. In the example of the passbook savings account, you *know* that your principal is insured by the FDIC or the FSLIC. That's a stated policy on the front door of all savings institutions that offer insured savings. In the case of rental real estate, however, assessing the risk of an investment is much more difficult. Housing values, for example, are determined by a very general set of criteria. This means that assessing the possible changes in the price of a certain property generally is less risky than, say, projecting the price of gold in five years. You have *knowledge* upon which to base your decision to buy or sell a particular property. As the saying goes, "Knowledge is power." The more knowledge you have about any investment you are considering, the better able you are to make a wise investment decision.

Many investors become frustrated because they cannot find the time to study investments. This is one reason why books that claim you can make sound investments with little time and effort sell so well. Unfortunately, many of these books are of little substance.

It cannot be stated strongly enough: *There is no quick and easy way to make sound investments.* To become knowledgeable about investments you must be willing to spend time doing your homework.

Unfortunately, *the stock market entails a high level of risk when compared with other investment alternatives. The reason is simply that you do not have any control over the market's movements or the changes in the price of individual stocks.*

Becoming *knowledgeable* about the underlying causes of stock market movements is more difficult than becoming knowledgeable about real estate, antiques, certificates of deposit, or passbook savings accounts. To understand stock market movements, you must understand how to analyze a company's financial performance, and that analysis needs to be updated as market and economic conditions change. Clearly, you are a bystander and have no control over other investors or the actions taken by any company's management which might affect that company's stock price. Therefore, your analysis must be kept current.

This lack of any form of personal managerial control contrasts with other forms of investment. In real estate, for example, you, as owner, can spend your time and money upgrading your property to secure higher rents. You control this decision. *When purchasing securities, and common stock particularly, you are not a major player in the game and exert virtually no control over your investments.* You have a limited number of choices: purchase, sell, or hold securities. That's it. Nonetheless. common stock represents a most popular form of investment, and you can profit from sound investment in stock and other securities. *Studies show that the patient stock market investor has outperformed investors who limit their portfolios to risk-free securities.*

STOCK MARKET ANALYSIS

> *"Isn't it strange? The same people who laugh at gypsy fortunetellers take economists seriously."*
>
> Cincinnati Inquirer

Why is it difficult to understand the movements of the stock market? Primarily because no body of knowledge precisely explains or governs the movement of stocks. Many very talented people have spent their lives trying to predict market movements and the movements of individual stocks. If you look at any issue of *Barrons,* one of the major investment newspapers, you will see many advertisements for various investment services: "Wave Theory," "Value Line," "Moody's," and many others. Each claims to provide you with special approaches for evaluating particular stocks or market movements.

Although the vast majority of these services are well accepted and respected by the investment community, they often vary greatly on what we might call the "philosophy" of how the market works. Some, like "Value Line," offer what is called *fundamental advice*. The assumption underlying the fundamental approach is simply that the action of the market is governed by the fundamentals of the companies and industries represented by the companies' stocks: sales, profits, debt, industry competition, and so on. Others, like the "Wave Theory," are *technical approaches* to the market. Technical analysts look for basic trends in the movement of prices and volume of stocks. By observing various patterns of movement, one can, according to this approach, predict when the stock market or a given stock will increase or decrease in price.

Fundamental and technical analysis may sound simple enough. In fact, these approaches are complicated and by no means easy to understand. Whole academic courses and programs are offered on securities analysis; certainly this is not something the average person can pick up in an evening's reading. However, we will provide you with an introduction to both methods of analysis later in this chapter which you can use as a foundation for further study.

Beyond analysis, however, the stock market remains as much a matter of *experience* as one of formal training in market theory. If you are willing to spend the time—perhaps ten to 15 hours each week—you may be in a position to minimize your risk in trading securities. Clearly, your *knowledge* of the stock market and of particular securities must be based heavily on your experience in actual trading, combined with study.

What if you are not willing to spend this amount of time? You still have three avenues open to you. First, you can seek the services of a financial planner or Registered Investment Advisor. This person should be a specialist in securities who offers investment advice on a fee basis—typically a percentage of the value of the portfolio of assets he or she manages. We recommend a person who is registered with the Securities and Exchange Commission (SEC) under the 1940 Federal Securities Act, or who is a member of the Institute of Certified Financial Planners.

Second, you can seek the services of a stock broker, typically associated with the large investment firms. A note of caution here. Unless you have a very large account and trade actively, you may not get the most experienced help. Not infrequently, smaller accounts end up with the less experienced salespeople in the big-name brokerage houses. This may or may not be a satisfactory situation, depending obviously on the skill of the individual. Again, your experience will be very important. If you are to minimize your risk, you will have to monitor your account carefully and not depend solely on the brokerage house's recommendations.

Finally, you can participate in a mutual fund, a choice millions of people make. What is a mutual fund? As noted in Chapter 4, mutual funds are associations of shareholders who own shares in the fund's total share of stocks, bonds, or other securities. Mutual fund portfolio managers buy and sell securities, just like you might, from a variety of industries and government agencies. This money is pooled, and shares, or fund units, are sold to individuals just like you and me. You can think of a mutual fund as a kind of derivative of the stock market—a market behind the market, so to speak.

The chief advantages of mutual funds are diversity and management expertise. Mutual funds tend to buy broadly or limit themselves to certain industry groups or governmental sectors (some funds are quite specialized, investing in precious metals or bonds). In so doing, they can concentrate on an industry and still spread the risk by owning securities of many companies. At the same time, mutual funds provide a level of sophistication in buying and selling often beyond the individual investor's capability. Of course, there is a cost. Investment managers charge for their services, and they are not always right!

FUNDAMENTAL ANALYSIS

"Enthusiasm without knowledge is like running in the dark."

Thousands of articles and dozens of books have been written on security analysis. As noted earlier, some of the more important materials you should read are included in Chapter 9. We hope that you will consider the approach described in this section as a first step and continue to read and develop investment expertise.

We explained earlier that *market analysis falls into two broad categories: fundamental and technical analysis.* Fundamental analysts look at a particular company in a particular industry and try to determine present financial performance and structure in order to predict changes in the market price of its stock.

In this section, we provide guidance for fundamental analysis. One of the authors is a Registered Investment Advisor who manages accounts totaling several million dollars. The methodology for fundamental analysis presented on the following pages is the system he uses to select stocks for purchase. This system is called "filtering." The financial statements of common stocks are reviewed and a series of ten "filters" or acceptance criteria are applied. The results of applying these filters leads to a profile of a company's common stock. The profile then is used to make a buy, sell, or hold decision.

In our investment experience, three basic factors are especially important when projecting a stock's performance:

- Low price-to-earnings ratio
- Low volatility
- High dividend yield

We consider these, along with seven other factors, when purchasing stock. You can use the ten filters described below to help you select stocks for your portfolio.

Low Price/Earnings (PE) Ratio

The PE ratio tells you how many dollars the market is willing to pay for a company's earnings. For example, if a stock has a market price of $50 per share, and its earnings-per-share are $5, then the PE ratio is ten to one. We look for stocks with PEs not exceeding the market average. Average PE ratios are available from stock brokers.

When the PE ratio is far above the average for the industry, investors are indicating exceptional optimism about the firm's future earnings. A high PE ratio indicates that investors as a group expect earnings to rise in the future. If investor expectations are not fulfilled, the price of the stock surely will tumble. *Numerous studies have shown that stocks with generally low PE ratios consistently outperform those with high PE ratios.*

Volatility

We tend to avoid stocks that exhibit wide swings in price relative to the movement of the overall market. A stock's volatility is measured by what is called its "beta" value. If the beta value is greater than one, the price of the stock is *more* volatile than the overall market (as measured by a broad-based index such as the Standard and Poor's 500 Stock Index).

Fundamental Analysis

When the beta value is below one, the stock is *less* volatile than the overall market.

For example, suppose you are considering a stock with a beta of 1.5. If the stock market as a whole increased or decreased by 10 percent, you could expect the price of that particular stock to increase or decrease by one and one-half times that amount, or 15 percent. If the stock had a beta of 0.5, you could expect the price to increase or decrease by only 5 percent. We prefer stocks with lower beta values—and especially so if we are using them as part of a covered call option writing program, to be described shortly. Beta values, incidentally, are readily available from stock brokers and financial literature.

Dividend Policy

We prefer stocks that pay dividends. Although dividend payment is not essential to our selection, we look for stocks that pay at least a 3 percent dividend. Also, since the elimination of the preferential treatment of long-term capital gains under the Tax Reform Act of 1986, dividends are increasingly more desirable.

Liquidity

We have described liquidity in previous chapters. Liquidity is also important for corporations, since it refers to the company's ability to pay its bills in a timely manner without having to incur additional debt. We measure liquidity using a financial ratio called the *acid test*. To compute the acid test ratio, you start with a firm's current assets and subtract inventories (inventories are not very liquid and therefore cannot be used to pay bills). You then divide the difference by the firm's current liabilities. *We look for companies with an acid test ratio of one or greater.* Firms exhibiting this level of liquidity tend not to need additional debt to finance their operations.

Stable or Growing Inventory Turnover

Inventory turnover is the ratio of sales to inventory. A company that exhibits a stable or increasing ratio of sales to inventory generally is retaining or increasing its market share (the company's market niche is intact). The marketing efforts continue to be successful, and the products are still being accepted.

Unlike the acid test ratio, where we seek firms with a ratio of one or more, we do not have a particular number to look for when computing the ratio of sales to inventory. Since the ratio of sales to inventory varies so much from industry to industry, using one particular number as a benchmark for comparison is not possible. Industry averages, however, are available from stock brokers, or you can visit your library and check a recent copy of *Robert Morris Statement Studies* or *Dun and Bradstreet*. Then compare the inventory turnover rates for the particular company you are analyzing with the industry averages. To this analysis we add an examination of a firm's financial statements over a period of years; we are looking for such trends as a stable or increasing ratio of sales to inventory.

Relatively Low Debt

The use of debt results in the need for a company to pay interest and repay or refinance principal (the amount borrowed). If sales should decrease, the interest expense can drag earnings down, and the use of debt tends to make earnings much more volatile. Nonetheless, the use of some debt can enhance earnings. We don't want to purchase stock of companies that use large amounts of debt to purchase their assets. Companies in this category would be risky investments. We prefer companies that use a prudent amount of debt and with a ratio of total debt to total assets of 35 percent or less.

Superior and Consistent Return on Equity

Equity is the difference between the value of a company's assets and its debts. Equity represents the amount owned by the shareholders. The return on equity is simply the company's earnings after taxes, divided by its equity. As a minimum, we look for companies that have a return on equity at least equal to the current rate of interest paid on Treasury Bills (T-Bills). We prefer companies that have a return on equity in excess of the T-Bill rate, but, more importantly, we look for companies with a return on equity consistently equal or above the T-Bill rate for a number of years. We believe that consistency is very important.

Superior and Consistent Return on Sales

Return on sales, or net profit margin, is obtained by dividing sales into earnings after taxes. *We look for companies that consistently show a return on sales of 4 percent or more.* Studies clearly demonstrate that companies which consistently provide a 4 percent or greater return on sales represent superior investments. You may believe that 4 percent, or four cents of earnings after taxes for each dollar of sales, sounds very low. Many people are under the false impression that companies make 20 or 30 cents from each dollar of sales. This is a fallacy. A consistent 4 percent return on sales is superior.

Sustained Earnings Growth

We look for companies that have sustained yearly earnings growth rates exceeding the current PE ratio. Rates of growth on earnings change over time. Therefore, you must go back several years to determine the average rate of earnings growth. Then compare the company's current PE with the growth in earnings for the past five years. If the average yearly growth in earnings exceeds the current PE ratio, the stock represents a superior investment.

Market Value Not Greatly Exceeding Book Value

The market value of the company is the market price per share multiplied by the number of shares outstanding. Thus, if a company's stock is selling for $30 per share, and there are 1,000,000 shares outstanding, then the market value is $30,000,000. The book value is the value of the company's assets less its liabilities and any preferred stock. *We look for companies that have a ratio of market to book value of 1.5 or less.*

Sometimes finding stocks that conform to all of these guidelines is very difficult and time consuming. When this is the case, we advise you to stay out of the stock market.

Two other factors can sway our decision about a potential stock purchase. First, whenever a company announces a *stock repurchase plan,* we take that to mean that the company's management, who obviously is in the best position to know, thinks the stock is currently underpriced. We always view such situations as possible signals to buy. Second, we always examine the *insider buy-sell decisions.* Insiders include a company's managers, board members, and major shareholders. If insiders are buying the stock, we tend to think that's a good omen.

Finally, we recommend a basic technical analysis once a stock meets the fundamental criteria just described. This process is described in the following section.

TECHNICAL ANALYSIS

Technical analysis examines market trends, frequently using charts and graphs, with the goal of predicting when major stock market movements will occur. Technical analysis is also used to predict a particular stock's future price trends based upon recent trading patterns. Technical analysts tend to fall into one of two groups. Some follow current price trends, while others follow current trading volume trends. Some follow both. The goal is to predict future price movement based on the history of price movements or trading volume changes.

Technical analysts who follow *price trends* use graphs and are called "chartists." They believe that certain frequently occurring sequences in price changes are reliable predictors of future price movements. When graphed, these patterns of price changes have been given such names as "head and shoulders," "pennants," "triple tops," "resistance break outs," and many others. Academic researchers have never been able to validate statistically the correlation between past price changes and the future changes which chartists predict. Nevertheless, every major investment firm has a technical analysis department, and the predictions made by chartists are closely monitored by institutional investors.

Technical analysts who follow *volume trends* attempt to determine whether institutional investors (such as bank trust departments, insurance companies, pension funds, and mutual funds) are currently buying or selling certain stocks. When institutions begin a pattern of buying a certain company's stock (called accumulation), they frequently tend to do so en masse. This is called the "herd instinct."

Following a combination of volume and price patterns can help to predict how the price of a company's stock may move in the future. For example, suppose a pattern of heavy volume on those days when the price of stock increases (up days) and light volume on down days is frequently observed over a period of a month. Such a trading pattern is called an *accumulation pattern*. Based on this pattern of purchasing, our experience indicates that the price of the company's stock will increase in the future. The technical analyst does not care to know why the issue is being accumulated, only that it is.

Volume technicians present diverse arguments explaining the bases of their projections. One of the more interesting arguments they put forth is based upon the elementary economic principle of supply and demand. As institutions accumulate many shares of a company's stock, the number of shares remaining available for daily trading shrinks. As with any other economic or financial commodity, as supply erodes, the price tends to increase.

The reverse of an accumulation pattern is called a *distribution pattern*. This occurs when institutional portfolio managers are removing (i.e., selling) a certain issue from their portfolios. It is characterized by heavy volume on down days and light volume on up days. A distribution pattern is thought to be a forerunner of a significant price drop for the stock in question.

Since the research that leads to an accumulation or distribution by an institutional investor frequently is proprietary, it is unavailable to the average investor. Consequently, we recommend a thorough fundamental analysis using the ten-part filter described earlier. When you find a company that exhibits a financial profile meeting all of the fundamental requirements, examine its volume/price trading for the past month. This can be accomplished by reviewing newspapers for the last month at your local library. Look for companies exhibiting an accumulation volume/price sales pattern and avoid companies exhibiting a distribution pattern.

We cannot guarantee that following our suggestions for fundamental and technical analysis will lead you to finding winners on a consistent basis, but it has proven useful and profitable for us.

COVERED CALL OPTION-WRITING PROGRAM

"Exhilaration is that feeling you get just after a great idea hits you and just before you realize what's wrong with it."

One way to enhance your return on common stocks is to utilize a *covered call option selling program,* also known as "covered call writing." This program is based on the use of call options. A call option is the right to purchase 100 shares of a particular stock during a specific period of time at a prespecified price (called the strike price).

Many people believe that options are risky. We agree! *Purchasing call options is a fool's paradise.* A person may purchase a call option, and if the price of the stock exceeds the strike price, a profit may be realized. In fact, most options expire and are never exercised. *The odds clearly favor those who sell call options, not those who purchase the options.*

We have found that one of the most conservative ways to obtain uncommonly high rates of return on discretionary investments is an active covered call option writing program. To demonstrate how a covered call option writing program works, consider the following example. Suppose XYZ Corporation's common stock trades for $40 per share. It meets our fundamental and technical analysis requirements and is a mature, well-managed company in an attractive industry. XYZ pays a *quarterly dividend* of $.50 per share ($2.00 per year) for a current yield of 5 percent. (The current yield is the annual dividend divided by the current price.) Suppose further that you purchase 100 shares of XYZ.

XYZ has call options listed on one of the organized options exchanges. You note a call option that expires in three months and has a strike price of $45. XYZ currently is trading at $40 per share.

For $80, plus a commission charge, a speculator could purchase a call option giving him or her the right—not the obligation—to purchase 100 shares of XYZ common stock any time within the next three months for $45 per share. This right would be extremely valuable if XYZ's common stock were to soar well above $45 per share during the period. Obviously, the call option would become worthless if XYZ's common stock did not exceed $45 per share by the time the option expires. The speculator who purchases the option is gambling $80 plus the commission fee that the price of XYZ will exceed $45 per share. If it does not, the speculator loses his or her money.

As the owner of 100 shares of XYZ common stock, you can *sell* a three-month call option on your shares of XYZ for $80, less commission. Since most call options expire (and the speculators lose their money), selling call options can add to your return. Obviously, *a covered call option writing program is likely to be useful when the stock market is relatively stagnant.* In an up market (bull market), the probability of the market price exceeding the strike price increases, and therefore you may

Covered Call Option-Writing Program

have to sell your stock more frequently. You also might miss out should the stock exhibit a dramatic price increase in a short period. Even so, you will have made a substantial profit.

Consider the implications of a call option on your 100 shares of XYZ common stock. First, once you sell the option, you would receive the $80 paid by the speculator for the option, less your broker's commission. Second, during the three-month period, you would receive XYZ's dividend of $50 on your 100 shares (unless the call option is exercised by the speculator before the strike date, which seldom occurs. If it did, then you immediately would receive $45 per share for your stock, which you must sell.) If the stock *does not* reach $45 per share during the three-month period, the option would expire, and you would retain your stock. You then would be able to sell another call option for potential additional income. As long as a speculator does not exercise the right to purchase the stock, you can continue to sell options every three months.

If the price of XYZ's stock were to exceed $45 per share, you would be forced to sell your stock to the speculator for $45 per share—*no matter how much higher than $45 per share the price of the stock might rise.* You would enjoy a profit, however, since you purchased XYZ for $40 per share. This profit would be the sale price of $4,500 less your purchase price of $4,000, or $500, before commissions.

If you bought 100 shares of XYZ's stock at $40 per share and sold one three-month $45 call option for $80, you would realize one of two possible rates of return: a static rate of return or a full-move rate of return.

The *static return rate* is the rate you would receive if the option expired. Referring to the example of XYZ stock, you obtained $80, less commission, when you sold the call option, and you also received a $50 dividend. Assume the commission on the sale of the option was $20, so that the net amount you received from the sale of the option was $60. You paid $4,000 to purchase the stock, plus commission. Assume that the commission on the purchase was $75, so that your total investment was $4,075. You would have received a total return during the three-month period of $60 + $50 = $110 on a $4,075 investment. This equates to an *annual return* of 10.8 percent.

Next, consider a *full-move rate of return*. Assume that the price of XYZ's stock appreciates during the three-month period beyond $45 per share, and you sell your stock to the speculator for $4,500. You now have a $500 gain, less commission, to add to your dividend and the net amount you received when you sold the call option. Assume that the brokerage fee on the sale of 100 shares of XYZ for $4,500 is $80, giving you a net of $4,420.

Your gain is calculated as follows:

Gain on sale of stock ($4,420 − $4,075)	$345
Sale of call option less commission	60
Dividend	50
TOTAL	$455

Your gain for three months would be $455 on a $4,075 investment, which is 11.2 percent. Annualized, the return is 44.8 percent. But don't expect that high a return on a consistent basis!

If the price of XYZ's stock appreciates to a value somewhere between $40 and $45 at the end of the option period, you would have an interesting opportunity. Suppose the price at the end of the three-month period is $43 per share. Not only would you be able to sell another $45 option, but you also would probably receive more than $80 for it. Since the price of XYZ's common stock would be closer to $45 than it was three months ago, a speculator would pay more for the $45 option, perhaps $130. You might choose, however, to sell an option with a *higher strike price* (such as $50) for a lower amount, perhaps $60. The $50 option would sell for a lower price than the $45 option because the probability that the price of XYZ's stock will exceed $50 in three months is much less than its exceeding $45. You could continue to sell options on your stock every three months until an option is exercised. Then you would have to sell the stock.

The covered call option writing program just described has the potential for enhancing your return on investment in the stock market. The example given is far from exceptional, nor is it contrived. *The options markets are terribly inefficient. Purchasing call options is tantamount to gambling at a casino.* The casino gambler may win, but over time, the casino always comes out ahead. Selling options, on the other hand, is akin to owning the casino!

Options markets have become the breeding ground for speculators lured by the prospect of incredible profit potential for a limited predetermined risk. The speculator's risk is the amount he or she pays for the option. Fortunately, the odds are heavily and disproportionately against speculators who purchase call options. You may be able to profit from selling call options to speculators.

Finding the right stock to write options against is the key to a successful program. Never, repeat *never,* purchase a stock to use in a covered option writing program simply because its options seem to be priced extremely high. Always select stocks based on their own merits, regardless of any option writing considerations. We recommend following the fundamental and technical analysis described earlier in this chapter as the basis for purchasing common stocks.

Within the ten-part fundamental filter described earlier, we recommend a value-based approach to stock selection. In particular, we recommend the selection of stocks with low price/earnings ratios and low beta values for use in a covered call option writing program.

Finally, *option writing programs help you make one of the most difficult investor decisions—at what price to sell your stock.* The undisciplined investor, seeing a significant price run-up in a stock, might not be sure if it's time to sell. A premature sale, after all, might mean missing out on a further upward move. Frequently, however, the stock slowly retreats to its previous level. Participating in a call option writing program can eliminate this problem. Once you have sold an option, you have committed yourself to a selling price. If the strike price of the option represented an attractive selling price at the beginning of the option period, stick with it. Let the stock go if the price exceeds the strike price. Don't buy back the option in an attempt to make a greater profit. Remember, the bulls get theirs, the bears get theirs, but the pigs get none!

Covered call option writing works best when the stock market is not volatile—when there is little movement. Although covered call option writing can enhance your return, you may not want to write options against all of your stocks. If, for example, you believe that the price of a stock will skyrocket, writing a call option on it doesn't make sense. Moreover, you may want to retain some stocks because you believe the long-term potential is excellent. You don't have to write call options against all your stocks. But it certainly can enhance your overall return.

MUNICIPAL BONDS

Although the bulk of this chapter has been devoted to a conservative approach to stock analysis and the use of call option writing, this section explains how you may use municipal bonds to enhance your overall return.

A municipal bond is a bond issued by a governmental unit, such as a state, county, city, or port authority. The proceeds of municipal bonds are used to fund a wide variety of public projects such as schools, housing for the elderly, hospitals, and turnpikes. Municipal bonds are generally sold in $10,000 denominations and pay interest semi-annually until maturity.

The interest paid to a municipal bond holder may not be subject to federal income tax. This evolves from a constitutional principle that the federal government is prohibited from taxing the various states. In everyday terms, this means that municipalities can fund projects at a lower cost than would be the case for a corporation. The tax-free treatment of most municipal bonds means that they will be attractive to investors even if yields are lower than comparable quality corporate bonds, CDs, Treasury securities, and the like. Check with your securities broker to determine which municipal bonds will be exempt from federal tax.

Additionally, many states exempt the interest paid by municipal bonds issued within that state from state income tax for residents of that state. If, for example, you live in New Jersey and purchased municipal bonds issued by a governmental unit within New Jersey, the interest from those bonds would not be subject to either Federal or state income taxes. Some limitations do exist, however. Discuss the purchase of any municipal bonds you are considering with your accountant to determine if you will be liable for any income tax on the interest received.

You should consider the following four factors before purchasing municipal bonds:

1. The bond's yield
2. The bond's grade (to be discussed)
3. The yield currently available from alternative taxable investments (CDs, corporate bonds, and so on)
4. Your marginal tax rate

Your marginal tax rate must be distinguished from your average (or effective) tax rate. Your average tax rate is simply the amount of tax you pay divided by your taxable income. This rate is not relevant to the purchase of municipal bonds. *Your marginal tax rate is the rate you will pay on any additional dollars of taxable income.* Beginning in 1988, most readers will have a 28 percent marginal tax rate.

Municipal Bonds

To determine if a municipal bond is preferable to another investment, you must compare the after-tax yields of the various alternative securities. This can be accomplished easily by multiplying the yield of a taxable security by the number one minus your marginal tax rate, as in the following example.

Suppose you have a 28 percent marginal tax rate and that you can buy a municipal bond that yields 7.5 percent (the bond is being issued for $10,000 and has semi-annual interest payments of $375). In addition, assume that comparable taxable securities are currently yielding 9 percent. You need to know if the taxable security has an after-tax return at least equal to the 7.5 percent tax-free return from the municipal bond. Simply multiply the 9 percent return by the number one minus your 28 percent marginal tax rate [9 percent (1 − .28) = 6.48 percent].

Since the after-tax return of the taxable security is 6.48 percent, the municipal bond yielding 7.5 percent tax-free is preferable. We conclude that the municipal bond is preferable to any taxable security yielding 9 percent, assuming, of course, that the investments are of comparable risk.

Municipal bonds come in two types—revenue bonds and general obligations. Revenue bonds (typically issued by turnpikes or other revenue-generating projects) are those whose interest payments are funded by revenues generated by the funded project. Many have provisions forcing bondholders to accept proportionately reduced interest payments in the event of a revenue shortfall. Consequently, *revenue bonds entail some risk.*

General obligation bonds can be used to fund projects that do not generate revenues—a city park, for example—as well as some projects that do generate revenues. *General obligation bonds are backed by the taxing authority of the governmental authority that issued the bond.* For example, a city might propose to its citizens (in the form of a referendum) that the city issue a general obligation bond to build a recreation center. If the bond issue passes, property taxes must be raised at any time during the life of the bond when interest payments are threatened by insufficient municipal revenues. Under certain circumstances, however, even the interest payments from general obligation bonds can be threatened (dwindling population, for example).

Municipal bonds are rated by Standard and Poor's Corporation and Moody's Investment Service. Municipal bonds may be an excellent investment vehicle for your discretionary capital, but stick to those bonds that are rated A or higher.

Municipal Bond Unit Trusts provide another way for investors to invest in municipal bonds. A Municipal Bond Unit Trust is a diversified portfolio of municipal bonds purchased by a brokerage firm. The brokerage firm sells shares to investors who then become part owners of the total portfolio of bonds. Interest is usually available to investors monthly, quarterly or semiannually, thereby providing the investor with an income stream meeting his or her individual needs.

A Municipal Bond Unit Trust differs from a mutual fund consisting of municipal bonds in that Unit Trusts are not managed by a portfolio manager. Once the portfolio of bonds is established, the portfolio is not altered until, of course, the bonds mature.

Interest payments received from Unit Trusts are subject to the same tax laws as government municipal bonds. The primary advantage of the Unit Trust is diversification. As a part owner of a Unit Trust, you own a piece of a diversified portfolio, which is less risky than purchasing individual issues of municipal bonds. But there is a cost. Administrative fees are deducted so your rate of return will be slightly reduced.

LET'S SUM UP

Investing in securities, especially corporate common stock, is the most popular form of investment. If you follow the techniques for analyzing stock described in this chapter, you likely will obtain higher than average returns. But you must do your homework regularly and never rely on "tips." When developing your security portfolio, remember to maintain adequate liquidity and diversity. Also, never become piggish. No one ever lost money taking profits. When you make a profit on the sale of a stock, rejoice. Don't gamble that you might make an even larger profit by "holding on just a little longer."

Covered call option-writing programs can add to your return. Since the options markets are so inefficient, selling covered options when the market is not too volatile may add to your profit.

For those who are hesitant to enter the stock market or who have a high marginal tax rate, municipal bonds may offer an above average return. Many municipal bonds are free of both federal and state tax and therefore warrant your consideration.

7

INVESTING IN YOUR OWN BUSINESS AND RENTAL REAL ESTATE

"Some people regard private enterprise as a predatory tiger to be shot. Others look on it as a cow they can milk. Not enough people see it as a healthy horse pulling a steady wagon."

winston churchill

Many people have supplemented their incomes and even become wealthy by operating their own businesses. We are not suggesting that you give up your job and go into business. Rather we are suggesting that by capitalizing on a hobby, interest, or skill you can invest in yourself and operate a part-time business out of your home. Each of the authors operates a part-time business out of his home. One provides financial counseling and securities management services; another operates a small publishing business, while the third manages rental real estate and a mail order business. One of the author's wives is considering making and selling crafts. In each case, some initial financial investment was required, but the results have been very rewarding. Here are some of the points you will want to note as you consider owning and managing your own business:

- The great opportunities afforded to those who operate businesses out of their homes
- How you can make thousands of dollars each year in a business and *legally* avoid paying taxes on much of the income
- What it is like to own and manage rental property
- Common misconceptions about property management
- Hints in purchasing rental properties
- Some important and frequently overlooked items to include in leases
- Selecting and keeping good tenants

WHY INVEST IN YOUR OWN BUSINESS?

"If you want to launch big ships, you have to go where the water is deep."

The principal reason to invest in your own business is to capitalize on your interests and control your investment. Many people believe that they are not smart enough to manage a business. This is not so. Owning and operating a part-time business can be very rewarding and need not be complicated. Yes, you may need occasional assistance from an accountant (to help you set up a bookeeping system and complete your tax returns) and a lawyer (to make sure you are meeting any state or local requirements).

Many people hesitate to invest in their own business because they believe that they lack management or marketing skills. These skills can be acquired; you don't need an MBA to operate a business successfully. They key element to operating any business successfully is a business plan. Writing a business plan does take time. *Investing in your own business is similar to making other investments—knowledge is power*, and to obtain the knowledge, you must do your homework. Chapter 9 provides the sources of information you need to get started writing a business plan without spending a lot of money.

A BUSINESS IN YOUR HOME—THE GREAT TAX ADVANTAGES

Some people think that the great tax advantage of operating a business out of your own home is cheating on your income taxes—becoming a part of the "underground economy." This is just not true. We do not advocate cheating on your taxes—it really isn't necessary! Why? Simply because the tax laws permit you legally to deduct all of your expenses, including some that you would have even if you didn't have a business. To understand this process, consider the following example.

You are interested in making crafts and selling them at flea markets. Over the past few years, you have been making them as gifts for birthdays and holidays. You decide to go into business. You set aside a portion of your basement for the exclusive and regular manufacture of the crafts. You decide to use existing tools and work benches, and you set aside a spare room as an office and a display area for sales. You also decide that you will need a desk and some power tools. You spend $500 to get the equipment you need for your business. This is tax deductible, as well as a portion of the costs for your home—specifically, those for your workshop, sales area, and office.

You own an automobile and now will use it for your business (to pick up supplies or go to flea markets). So part of your automobile expenses will be tax deductible.

What kinds of costs are tax deductible?

A Business in Your Home—The Great Tax Advantages

- Supplies
- Electricity to operate your workshop and office (including air conditioning)
- Heat for your workshop and office
- Maintenance for your workshop and office
- Part of the exterior maintenance of your home (for example, part of the cost of painting your home)
- The part of your homeowner's insurance attributable to the business portion of insurance coverage for the tax year
- Cleaning services for your office and shop
- Depreciation on those portions of your home used as workshop and office
- Postage, stationery, and other expenses related to your business
- Part of your telephone bill
- A mileage deduction or a portion of the actual expenses incurred to operate your automobile, including depreciation, insurance, interest on auto loans, gasoline, repairs, and so on
- Depreciation of any new or used equipment for your business
- The interest paid on any loans to finance equipment
- Entertainment expenses related to your business (Note that only 80 percent of such expenses may be deducted.)
- Food and beverages you consume while you are away from home overnight on business trips
- Motel or campsite costs when you are on the road selling your crafts
- Part of the cost of operating and maintaining a trailer if you use it to transport your crafts or sell crafts from it
- Depreciation on a trailer used in your business
- Part of your property taxes and mortgage interest expenses

This list goes on! You probably realize that many of the costs we listed are ones you already incur, such as heating your workshop or office, or costs you can't deduct, such as depreciation. You will need to do two things to take full advantage of the legal deductions available to you.

    1. Discuss your business and *all* its related costs with your accountant (preferably a CPA who specializes in taxes). The accountant will be able to tell you which expenses are deductible and how to maintain records of sales and expenses.

2. Keep very accurate records so that in the event you are audited, you will be able to substantiate your deductions.

Let's give an example. You deduct the cost of a three-day business trip to Camp Sun-N-Fun, including automobile expenses, meals, and lodging. You need to itemize the expenses (with receipts) and your sales when you are there. Obviously, you can't deduct $500 in expenses against $20 in sales; the primary purpose of the trip must be for business so you will have to do some selling if you expect to take full advantage of the tax breaks. Our experience indicates that most people can find $6,000 to $10,000 of expenses (not including the actual cost of their supplies) which they may deduct as legitimate business expenses if they operate a business out of their home and use their automobile in the business. But note the following:

1. *You must operate in a business-like manner, clearly indicating that your motive is profit.* Hobby expenses are not deductible.
2. *There are limits on deductions,* and, in particular, those having to do with an office or shop in the home. These deductions may not exceed the net income generated by the business.

Take another example: Suppose your sales are $10,000, and your actual operating expenses are $8,000. Your net income is therefore $2,000. Even if the cost of your home office and shop (including depreciation) is $5,000, you may deduct only $2,000 as home office and shop expenses. If your sales were $15,000 and operating expenses were $8,000, leaving $7,000 as net income, then you could deduct $5,000 in home office and shop expenses. The remaining $2,000 would be taxable income.

The tax advantages aren't over yet, however. If you aren't already employed and covered by a pension plan, you likely will qualify for an IRA. (See Chapter 5 for details on IRAs.) You may put $2,000 of your business profits into an IRA. If you don't qualify for an IRA, you may be able to place approximately 20 percent of any profits into a retirement plan of your own. Your accountant can provide you with the details of these other plans.

Operating a business out of your home can be a profitable and rewarding experience. Millions of people have small businesses, many of which have grown into full-time enterprises, providing employment for spouses and children as well. Then there is another important advantage to investing in your own business: You own and manage it! You are in control, making daily decisions, not just being a passive bystander!

INVESTING IN REAL ESTATE

In the middle of the Depression a landlord was summoned by the vice president of his bank. "About that $300,000 loan . . . ," the banker began.
The landlord interjected, "Mr. Jones, what do you know about property management?"
The banker answered, "Nothing."
"Better learn fast," advised the landlord, "you're in it."

Purchasing and managing real estate is probably the most popular type of part-time business. Many people have become wealthy by investing in rental real estate, but it does require work and is not for everyone. The remaining sections of this chapter are written by the author who has owned and managed several multiple-family dwellings and garages over the past 15 years.

If you want to get rich using other people's money in real estate, you can run to your local bookstore and buy one or more of at least 50 books claiming to explain the secrets of getting rich in real estate. You can attend seminars and buy cassettes to play in your car so you can learn all about real estate on your way to work.

The fact is that if there were so much money to be made so easily in real estate, no one would take the time to write books, conduct seminars, or sell cassettes telling you how to do it. These people would be out making a fast fortune and keeping the "secrets" to themselves.

In our opinion, must of what has been written and preached about real estate is simply "hype" and "hokum" designed to entice you not into buying real estate but purchasing books or cassettes. So save your money. You need not reach any further for the secrets of making money in real estate. The "secret" simply is this: *You can become wealthy in real estate if you are willing to spend the time, do the work, and put up with the aggravations.* Real estate management is a business, not a hobby or a free ticket to financial security. But by working hard and applying your managerial ability, you may be able to increase your wealth and become financially secure.

WHAT IT'S LIKE WHEN YOU OWN REAL ESTATE

You get home from work about 5:45 P.M. and play back the messages on your answering machine. The tenant in the Maple Avenue first floor efficiency apartment says that water is coming through the ceiling. You try to call him, but there is no answer. You call the plumber and find out he's on another job. So you ask your spouse to keep dinner warm, and you drive over to the apartment.

Water is indeed coming from the ceiling! You remove some of the drop-ceiling tiles but cannot find the exact source of the leak. You go upstairs where the tenant is fixing her dinner and tell her that you need to shut off the water to her sink because you think that it is the source of the leak. She grumbles about missing her dinner.

You proceed under the sink and remove the tenant's various pots, pans, and water-soaked paper bags, a box of soap powder and a box of scouring pads—all wet! You were right. The water was coming from the sink. The leak is in the joint between the pipe and the fixture, so you proceed to shut off the water. Would you believe there's no water shutoff valve in the line?

By now the tenant is really angry. Her kitchen looks like it was hit by a bombing raid; water is everywhere, and you just announced that you have to turn the water off in the entire building. You kiddingly suggest that the tenant call out for pizza, as you leave her apartment to turn off the water in the basement and to call the plumber.

It's now after 7:00 P.M. and the plumber is home. Fortunately, he has helped you out in the past, and since you have always paid him promptly, he says he will come over after dinner to fix the problem.

As it turns out, the faucets are beyond repair, and the plumber doesn't have a spare set in his truck. He installs a shut-off valve and turns the water back on for the building. Now it's 9:00 P.M., and he says he will return tomorrow to put in new faucets. Of course, the tenant works and so you lend the plumber your keys and arrange to pick them up later in the week.

After cleaning up the mess created by the leak, you arrive home at 9:30 P.M. Several ceiling tiles in the first-floor apartment have been water-soaked and stained. They will dry out, but you make a note to replace them. The phone rings, and you find yourself on the receiving end of a long gripe-list from the tenant whose apartment you had to turn topsy-turvy. She claims you ruined $12.00 worth of soap products and stained her new kitchen rug . . . and her kids got a cold dinner and had to go to bed late! You agree to let her deduct $12.00 from next month's rent.

You have *your* dinner at 10:00 P.M. Three days later the plumber's bill arrives: $125.00 for labor and materials. Not bad, considering he made two trips and replaced the faucets. Perhaps, if you were really handy, you could have made the repairs yourself and saved a few dollars. You also would have been home for dinner at 11:00 P.M.

From our experience, repairs are always ongoing. Tenants are demanding and sometimes do not meet their commitments, especially when it comes to paying their rent on time. Property management is not an easy business. Unlike the simple-minded picture painted in some of the real estate books, managing real estate is not a matter of purchasing property with no down payment and relaxing as tenants help pay off your mortgage.

REALITIES AND FALLACIES OF PROPERTY MANAGEMENT

Based on the author's experience and that of other landlords we know, we have assembled the basic principles of property ownership and management.

1. *You can make money in property management.* However, the Tax Reform Act of 1986 has sharply limited the tax advantages of real estate ownership which existed under prior law. Accelerated depreciation has been eliminated for real estate and the depreciable lives increased. Moreover, long-term capital gains have been eliminated. Finally, the tax deductibility of any losses incurred from real estate has been eliminated for many taxpayers.

2. *Rental real estate is very illiquid.* Although it is possible to attain financial independence and become wealthy by investing in real estate, you will find that you may not be able to spend the wealth. If you need cash, you can borrow using your real estate as collateral for the loan, but interest rates on such loans frequently are high, because lenders view them as business loans, not personal or home equity loans.

3. *Since rental real estate is illiquid and takes time to sell, it is especially important to maintain a diversified portfolio when you invest in real estate.* You should not put all your money into real estate. Moreover, you will want to consider maintaining ample life insurance coverage, especially if you have large mortgages. Finally, if you purchase real

estate, find properties in different towns. Should taxes rise sharply in one town or costly rent controls be imposed, you don't want to have all of your property located there. *Diversify by location of investment.*

4. *It is very difficult to make a profit without being personally involved.* It is true that professional property management companies will manage your real estate for you. But our experience has been that they are expensive and may be unreliable. To make money in property management you almost always have to show properties to prospective tenants, collect rents, pay bills, perform repairs, and sometimes go to court. This is not what the average person has in mind for the use of spare time, and the professionals do the job at professional prices!

5. *Purchasing properties takes time.* Our experience has been that it takes an average of three to six months to find a property that will meet our requirements. Normally we will drive by 30 to 40 properties and inspect a dozen before we make an offer. It's very unusual to find a single-family home that will produce rentals equal to your expenses. The person who can pay $1,000 per month for mortgage, taxes, water, sewer, and repairs probably is going to buy his or her own home—not rent from you. By contrast, two tenants who cannot afford to purchase their own homes might pay $500 each to rent the two halves of a duplex. Our purchasing requirements are discussed in the following section.

6. *Selling properties takes time and requires planning.* At some point you will want to sell. Unless you want to give your property to someone, expect to spend at least six months to find the right buyer. If, as some of the real estate books indicate, you can purchase property with no money down, then another property owner who wants to sell is probably having to take back a mortgage with little down payment in order to sell at a reasonable price. We would not recommend taking back a mortgage with little down payment. Why do some people do this, then? Simply because it is the only way they can move the property quickly at a reasonable price.

7. *You should have a business plan.* You need a plan outlining how much property you expect to buy, how you will rent the apartments, how it will be maintained, when you plan to sell it, and so on. Real estate is a business and needs careful planning, just like any other business.

8. *You will require legal assistance periodically and should employ an attorney who specializes in real estate.* Most states have laws that severely restrict the rights of landlords. These laws generally favor the tenants. Eviction procedures, for example, are usually lengthy and complicated. The "good old days" when you could put the tenant's belong-

ings on the front doorstep and change the locks are gone! Moreover, the typical stationery store rental agreement form may contain legally unenforceable clauses and omit ones that should be included. You definitely need legal assistance.

9. *Unless you are skilled and have a lot of time, you will need to develop dependable relationships with repairpersons and particularly a plumber and roofer.* You especially will need to find a trustworthy plumber who will make evening and weekend calls. Leaks can cost thousands of dollars if not repaired promptly!

10. *You need an answering machine and should have someone on call at all times.* Problems don't go away when you go on vacation. You need someone who can handle emergencies in your absence.

11. *You can obtain substantial financial leverage when purchasing real estate.* Real estate can be purchased with relatively small down payments. Our experience has been that you should expect to have about 10 percent minimum for a down payment, plus closing costs. This means you can purchase a property for $100,000 using only about $17,000 of your own money—perhaps even less.

12. *You will need to join or have access to a credit bureau.* You must run credit checks on applicants. Sometimes a local realtor will do this for about $10.00 cash. It's more convenient to become a member, however.

PURCHASING RENTAL PROPERTY

Expect to spend a lot of time finding a suitable rental property. As with buying your own home, find out all you can about the neighborhood and municipality in which you plan to invest. Refer to the guidelines for location outlined in Chapter 2. Then proceed with caution.

Purchase only those properties that have rental income sufficient to cover all operating costs plus mortgages and taxes. Sellers and real estate agents will tell you that you can make up losses resulting from expenses exceeding rentals in three ways. First, tax benefits may be available. This is true, but, as we have noted, the tax benefits of real estate ownership have been reduced substantially by the Tax Reform Act of 1986.

Second, they will say that simply because of inflation you will make a substantial profit when you sell. This may be true, but our view is that price increases resulting from inflation are a bonus. Remember that inflation is a double-edged sword. You may gain as a result of appreciation in property value, but you will have to pay more for upkeep and other expenses during periods of high inflation. We recommend, therefore, that appreciation from inflation not be included in the purchasing decisions. Third, they note that rents will go up. This may also be true, but so will expenses. Don't depend on next year's profits to offset this year's losses.

Expect expenses to be understated, especially for repairs. Many sellers will list expenses showing minimal repairs. Repairs, of course, will vary with the structure. We recommend brick, strucco, or aluminum (or vinyl) sided structures. Avoid wood. Painting is very expensive. As a rule, annual maintenance is about 3 to 5 percent of the fair market value of the property if you do some of the work yourself. Request that the seller verify expenses by producing tax, water, sewer, and other bills. Also request to see the section on the seller's income tax report which lists rents and expenses for the past two years.

Avoid properties with common heating, hot water, and electric service. Separating heating, hot water, and electrical service for each apartment allows tenants to assume responsibility for their own utilities. If you plan to purchase a property without separate utility services, obtain estimates of the cost to separate these utilities so that tenants will pay for their own utilities in the future. We recommend separating utilities immediately after you purchase a property and building this cost into your financial calculations.

Look for properties with low tenant turnover. Request to see existing leases and ask for a history of renters and vacancies. Turnover is very expensive. It normally requires repainting of the apartment, advertising, and sometimes the loss of a month's rent while the apartment is between tenants.

Look for properties with refrigerators and space available for a washer and dryer in a common area such as a basement. Most tenants don't have refrigerators; you will have to supply them. Tenants will pay added rent if a washer and dryer are available on the premises—frequently $20 to $30 per month. For larger apartment houses we recommend coin-operated units. For two- or three-unit apartment houses, consider less expensive, standard units and provide separate electric outlets for each apartment.

Check insurance costs. Liability insurance especially is becoming expensive for dwellings of three or more units. Also, the liability insurance on condominiums paid by the condo association (and reflected in the condo fee) may be quite high. Type of building construction can affect fire insurance costs. Don't depend on a seller's bills to reflect your costs.

Leases

The seller may not maintain adequate *replacement value* fire insurance or adequate liability insurance.

Avoid properties with many common areas such as stairs or halls. Requirements for smoke detectors and sprinkler systems often are stringent for such areas. We recommend looking for properties with hard-wired (not battery-operated) smoke detectors and which are certified as having met all fire code requirements.

Be sure the property meets zoning requirements. For example, some sellers will try to sell a house with a mother-in-law's apartment as a duplex. Be sure to check with the town zoning officer to be sure the property is zoned for such a use.

Be sure the property meets all state and local building, fire alarm (smoke detectors), building code, and other requirements. Your lawyer should incorporate a statement into the agreement of sale that the seller warrants the property to meet all such standards and will pay for any work required to bring the property into compliance with these standards.

LEASES

The lease is the contract between you and your tenant. A lease should always be in writing. We have several recommendations for leases:

A lease should be prepared by a lawyer who specializes in real estate. Once a *legal lease* is prepared, you can reproduce it and use it for many tenants.

Be sure to consider including clauses relating to the following when you discuss the lease with your lawyer:

- Additional rental payments if the rent is late
- Additional rental payments if the tenant gives you a bad check
- Prohibition of water beds (they are extremely heavy and can cause thousands of dollars damage if they should leak)
- Requirement that the tenant clean windows and storm windows at least once a year
- Snow removal and lawn maintenance (who does what)
- Need for tenant to maintain insurance on their possessions
- Security deposit (always get as much as allowed by statute)
- Subletting (don't permit it!)
- Damage (tenant pays for damage and litigation costs, if necessary)

- Locks (don't permit tenants to change them without your written permission)
- Access (you must be able to enter for inspection and repairs)
- Alterations (don't permit them)
- Disturbances
- Pets (don't allow them, or charge added rent if you do)
- Painting (encourage tenants to use one color paint in all your apartments, such as an antique white—semigloss for trim, flat for walls; using one color and brand of paint will save you a lot of money)
- Extras (note the curtains, drapes. and mirrors that remain part of the rental premises)

If a tenant vacates prior to the termination of lease, provide that (1) the tenant forfeits the security deposit and accrued interest; (2) the tenant will continue to pay rent until you have found another tenant; (3) the tenant will continue to pay utilities until you have found another tenant; and (4) the tenant will pay for advertising. Check with your lawyer to confirm the legality of these clauses in your region.

SELECTING AND KEEPING TENANTS

Good tenants can be a joy; bad tenants can break you. Selecting tenants is the most critical part of property management. We recommend the following:

1. *Use an application form.* Your lawyer can help you with this, but bascially you need three items: (1) Credit history—the name, address, employment, date of birth, and social security number of the applicant; (2) employment record--the name and address of employer, salary statement by applicant, and length of employment; and (3) landlord references.

We recommend that you charge a minimum of $20 to process the application. When prospective tenants call, explain that they will have to complete the application and pay the application fee. The fee is nonrefundable and *does not* guarantee that they will be accepted as tenants.

2. *Always check an applicant's credit with the credit bureau.* Usually an applicant who has bad credit will not waste your time to look at an apartment if he or she knows you will run a credit check.

3. *Always verify employment, salary, longevity, and potential for*

future employment. Employers will not normally divulge salary but will verify salary and other particulars if the applicant has listed them on the application. Employers may also comment on an applicant's cleanliness and financial responsibility.

4. *Always check with current and prior landlords.* You need to know whether the tenant paid his/her rent on time and whether the person maintains certain standards of cleanliness and respect for others' property.

Landlord references may be of minimal value, especially if the current landlord wants to get rid of the tenant. The current landlord may lie to you. Also, tenants may give a friend's name, and the friend may tell you a "dream story" about your applicant. The best way to determine how a prospective tenant lives is to visit him or her at their current residence. This maybe a nuisance to you, but it may save you a lot of grief later on!

5. *Always collect the maximum security deposit allowed by law.* Security deposits are seldom enough to pay for damage, so get what you can. Always obtain the security deposit and the first month's rent before giving a tenant the keys. Be sure to collect these amounts in cash, certified check, or money order. Personal checks can bounce. If an applicant doesn't have enough money to cover the security deposit and the first month's rent, you don't want that person as your tenant.

6. *When interviewing prospective tenants, look at their clothes, fingernails, shoes, and automobile.* If the applicant and his/her car is dirty, you can expect this person to keep a dirty apartment. Also, be sure the prospect owns a vacuum cleaner. Many people do not and will let the dirt accumulate.

7. *Avoid applicants who can move in tomorrow.* People who only require 24 hours to move in may require even less to move out! You don't want transients.

8. *If you have any doubt about an applicant's ability to pay the rent, but otherwise find the applicant acceptable, find a cosigner.* The cosigner should be a stable, financially secure person, preferably a parent who owns a home.

BEFORE YOU RENT YOUR APARTMENT, YOU ARE IN CONTROL. Once the lease has been signed, however, the tenant is in control. It is most difficult to evict tenants in many localities, and you certainly don't want to go through this aggravation. *Screen carefully!*

Once you have selected a tenant, request a deposit to hold the apartment. We recommend $200 minimum. The deposit guarantees that you will rent the apartment to the applicant. If the applicant changes his or her mind, the deposit is forfeited. Be sure to sign the lease and obtain the security deposit before the tenant moves in. As we have already noted, always request that the security deposit and first month's rent be remitted in cash, certified check, or money order. Personal checks may bounce.

Specify in the lease that the tenant is to pay you by check or money order. If the tenant pays by check, note the bank, branch, and account number. These may be useful later if litigation is necessary and you want to collect a judgment.

It pays to treat tenants well. You want to minimize turnover. When you are fortunate to have a good tenant, keep these in mind:

1. Minimize rent increases from year to year. Increase the rent when a tenant leaves. Naturally, you may have to make exceptions, such as for increased costs or other unforeseen circumstances. Explain these to your tenant.
2. Follow up rapidly on maintenance. Don't let the property run down.
3. Encourage the tenant to paint and do small repairs. Offer to reimburse the tenant for paint and other supplies if they will provide the labor. Explain that this will help to minimize rent increases.
4. Try to accommodate the tenant if he or she plans to move. When it is time to renew the lease, a tenant may indicate that a move may be necessary within a year and that a month-to-month lease will be needed. We recommend that you avoid month-to-month leases; rather, provide a year's lease with the right of the tenant to terminate with 60 days' notice. At the same time, negotiate an agreement whereby you may advertise and show the apartment before the tenant leaves.

The cooperation of a good tenant can make renting much easier. It is also far easier to rent an apartment which has furniture in it than a vacant one. Furthermore, if an apartment becomes vacant, you probably will have to paint it (all the dirt and holes will show). If an apartment is occupied, you may be able to get a prospective tenant to move in without painting—on the understanding that he or she will paint the apartment if you reimburse the cost of supplies.

LET'S SUM UP

Owning a business has helped millions of people reach financial independence. Having your own business can provide extra income needed to supplement your pension, pay off your mortgage, or eliminate those dreadful car payments. You control your investment. This is not to say that you won't make mistakes and lose money; you won't always operate at a profit. But you can learn from your mistakes and increase your success as you and your business grow. Consider contacting a trade association for extensive information on a business of your interest.

Although rental property management is very popular, it is not for everyone but does represent one way of attaining financial independence. If your work does not require that you travel and if you are capable of doing many repairs, property management should be considered. Of course, you don't want to place all of your money in real estate. Even though you may be successful at property management, you still want to maintain a diversified portfolio.

At this juncture, you probably have a solid plan for attaining your financial independence. With goals and priorities set, you are ready to move ahead. Before you commence, we suggest that you read Chapters 8 and 9. Chapter 8 talks about trusts and wills. You must have a will; don't delay on this. You also may want to consider a trust. Chapter 9 provides you with the ways to obtain necessary information about possible investments (everything from securities to starting your own business) at minimal cost. Remember, knowledge is power when it comes to making money!

8

ESTATE PLANNING

"Folks used to worry because they couldn't take it with them. In today's tax climate, their only worry is whether it will last as long as they do!"

Volumes have been written on estate planning. You certainly don't want to read them, and unless you are a lawyer, you probably wouldn't understand them anyway. Nevertheless, your financial security, as well as that of your family, demands that you spend some time planning your estate.

For most people, estate planning amounts to preparing a will, which we describe in the following section. Others may recognize the need to create a trust for their children or their spouse. Still others may forget about trusts altogether, feeling that such matters are only for the rich to worry about. In fact, nothing could be further from the truth, as we will show you in the section on trusts.

In this chapter we address these important areas relating to estate planning:

- Preparing and updating your will
- Selecting a lawyer
- Selecting an executor for your will
- Protecting your family and your estate by establishing a trust

Before we talk about estate planning, we would ask you to follow these guidelines:

1. Don't undertake estate planning on your own. *Utilize the services of a lawyer who specializes in estate planning.* The cost for a specialist may be little more than that for a "general practitioner," but the quality of the advice will be more than worth it. Also, if you are in business, contact your trade association for useful information on estate planning.
2. *Estate planning is an ongoing process.* As you acquire more wealth, raise children, or change your personal circumstances, your needs for estate planning will change. You should review and update your will and other documents at least every five years, and more often if a major change in your life has occurred.

3. *Tax considerations are important.* Remember that you will never be in a better position to pay taxes than when you die. It's true, your heirs will wind up paying them, not you. This is one of the major reasons why we encourage you to consult with a lawyer who specializes in estate planning. More on lawyers later in this chapter.

YOUR WILL*

The smooth processing of your estate depends critically on your will. Every person 18 years or older should prepare one. *A properly executed will is a legal directive on who gets what and how much.* Without a will, you risk leaving your heirs with financial insecurity and possible disharmony (how many times have we heard stories about family squabbles over the deceased's possessions?). And contrary to popular opinion, you need a will even if you have a very small estate.

What happens if you don't make a will? Your estate will be distributed by a court in accordance with state laws. This can be a cumbersome, time-consuming matter. But more important, your wishes may not be realized. The law will dictate who administers your estate and how your assets will be distributed. Without a will, you risk not being able to appoint the guardian of your choice for your children. Your property might even be distributed to people in whom you have no interest.

Here's one hard-and-fast rule to remember in preparing a will: Don't do it yourself! Consult a lawyer. In addition to determining your wishes, he or she will know all the legal and procedural technicalities that must be followed if the will is to be properly executed. This is no place for the amateur. People frequently ask if it is legal to make one's own will. Yes, it is. It is also legal to remove your own appendix, but we don't recommend it!

In making your will, be aware of these points:

- You don't need to make an itemized statement of your assets, nor do you need to state the disposition of your property item by item.
- You can change your will at any time you wish.
- Your will is not recorded before your death; no one need know of its contents, if that is your wish.

*Material for this section excerpted, with permission, from "A Will of Your Own," by Donald H. Wagner, Surrogate, Gloucester County, N.J.

- The existence of the will does not affect your ability to sell or dispose of property. You may continue as though you had not written it.

Start by making a list of everything you own and all you owe. In addition, list how the property is registered. For example, is your checking account in joint names or just in your name? Your lawyer will need to know this in order to properly advise you. Decide to whom you want to leave your real and personal property. Do this systematically. Be certain you have stated just what your wishes are by making a list of the persons involved, their relationship to you, your objectives, when the bequest is to be given, and how it is to be provided (for example, trust fund or life insurance trust). Also include the source of the funds (general estate or proceeds from insurance policies). Take this list to your lawyer.

SELECTING AN EXECUTOR

Next, select an executor, executrix, or personal representative to administer your will. This may be the beneficiary who will inherit the bulk of your estate, a member of your family, your legal or financial advisor, a trusted friend, or personal representative. You also should name an alternate to act in case your first selection should die prematurely or is unable to serve. Note that the executor, executrix, or other representative who administers your estate will receive a percentage of your estate. The amount is governed by law and may be around 5 percent. Note also that if a lawyer is used in addition to the executor, he or she will charge an additional fee or percentage of the estate. *We recommend payment on an hourly basis for actual legal services rendered rather than as a percent of the estate.*

A bank can act as executor, personal representative, trustee under a trust, or as a guardian of either a minor or an incompetent person. Some bank trust departments are experienced and familiar with accounting and management details.

The choice of your executor or personal representative and trustee should be made with great care. The discussion should be businesslike, not sentimental. Although sentiment and friendship cause some people to name members of the family or close friends, remember that your executor or personal representative has the important responsibility of settling your estate and seeing that the wishes expressed are faithfully carried out. If you have a trusted family attorney, he or she can be named as executor of your estate. The attorney's expertise in such matters can prove to be very valuable to the loved ones left behind.

BASICS OF TRUSTS

Many people believe that trusts are just for the rich, but this is *not* the case. Trusts should be considered if you have life insurance, own a business, or have a sizeable estate. One client has testamentary trusts (trusts under his will) for both his wife and daughter. Why?—simply for the preservation of assets and for security. When he nears retirement, he plans to establish a living trust to assure proper management of his assets in the event either he or his wife becomes incapacitated.

Like many people in business, he and his wife have little of their money invested in securities; the bulk is in a business. If he should die, the business probably would be liquidated to generate cash. Furthermore. large insurance and pension proceeds would be distributed to his wife and daughter. Without a trust, his wife would be faced with the problem of investing large sums of money—an area in which she has had minimal experience. Without doubt, there would be many who would offer his wife advice and try to sell her stock, limited partnerships, mutual funds, and half ownership in an electric fork! The client has discussed this problem and concluded that the interests of both his wife and daughter would be better served if the funds were placed in a trust.

Actually, we think the trust has provided her with as much peace of mind as it has for the client. She will not be faced with the problem of investing large sums of money in the event of his death. Keep in mind that the terms of the trust he has created meet his own family's needs, but they may not be suitable for someone else's family. *Trusts are extremely flexible and should be tailored to meet a particular family's needs.*

A trust can protect those you care about in many ways—from bad investment advice, from greedy children or grandchildren, from undue generosity on the part of the beneficiary, and from unfair pressure by clergy or charities. Trusts can perpetuate the name of the one who has died by serving as a reminder, when the income checks are received, that they are flowing from the accumulated life's savings of the trust's creator. Trusts can be reminders to beneficiaries for many years that the one who created the trust cared about them.

Basics of Trusts

Having actually set up trusts for ourselves, we want to share some of our experience with you. We don't want to give you legal advice or suggest how you should distribute your assets. Rather, we want to give you information on selecting a trustee and a lawyer and managing your trust.

Getting Started

As we pointed out earlier, *the first step in estate planning is preparing a list of all your personal and business assets and liabilities.* Include the properties you own individually and jointly and label them accordingly. For securities, indicate the date purchased, purchase price, and current market value. For real property (land and buildings), indicate the date purchased, purchase price, and current market value. If you are not certain about the market value, obtain appraisals. Take the time to inventory your safe deposit box and ascertain the paid-up value of your life insurance. Be sure to indicate the policy values of the life insurance and note the names of the current beneficiaries.

Taking an inventory of assets should not be used as an excuse to avoid meeting with the attorney or trust officer and getting the work started. Many people delay for years in the formulation of an estate plan because they want to tie down values more precisely or allow transactions to occur which they believe will simplify the plan.

We recommend that you consider involving your spouse and perhaps other beneficiaries in the estimation of your worth, and in the rest of estate planning as well. Consider bringing your spouse to meetings with the trustee and lawyer, especially if he or she takes an active role in business affairs.

After the trust is established, you may want to meet periodically with the trustee. Many trustees are flattered by a luncheon invitation, and meeting a trustee for lunch might be the way to establish a good contact which goes beyond the office. Your goal is to develop a personal relationship with the trustee. If you become physically incapacitated, you will need his or her assistance. Having a good relationship with a trustee will prove to be very valuable in the future.

The second step in establishing a trust is to select a trustee. Let's look at what's involved here.

Many people believe that only banks with trust departments or trust companies may act as a trustee. This is not true. Large stock brokers, for example, have trust departments you should investigate. You also might appoint a lawyer or other trusted person with investment experience to serve as a trustee. When an individual is appointed as a trustee, however, you must be concerned with continuity. What would happen if that individual were to die, become ill, or go on vacation? A corporate trustee provides continuity of administration, a significant advantage over any individual trustee.

You need to shop around to find the institution or person most suitable to your needs. Consider the following nine factors in making your selection:

1. *Location.* Since you and your surviving spouse and children will be dealing with the trustee, select one within 50 miles of your home if possible. Usually this is not difficult, unless you live in a rural area.

2. *Size.* If you choose a bank, consider selecting one with assets in excess of $250 million and with a separate trust department managed by a full-time trust service. In rural areas you may have to choose a smaller bank with assets of perhaps $40 million or more and a part-time trust staff. Some smaller banks may use a loan officer for part-time trust work. Since the work of a trustee is complex, you generally will be served better by people who specialize in the field. Look for an institution employing trust officers with law degrees, MBA's or master's degrees in taxation.

If your estate is not large (less than one million), you may want to avoid a very large bank or trust company. You and your heirs will need personal service from someone who recognizes your name when you call. When visiting trust departments, ask about the average size of trusts they manage. If these are much larger or smaller than yours, consider looking further.

3. *Interest and willingess to meet your needs.* Most trust offices have a "new business person." This person should be willing to meet with you and discuss your needs and how the trust department can meet them without any charge or obligation on your part. The person should appear knowledgeable and be willing to answer any questions you may have about the trust department, including charges and methods of reporting transactions. Additionally, you may want to speak with someone in the trust department who is involved with estate or trust administration.

4. *Your commercial bank or another institution?* All other things being equal, selecting the trust department in the same bank that you use for your checking account and commercial loans may be advantageous.

Basics of Trusts

First, since you are an established customer, you may receive better service. Second, lines of communication may be a little less formal. If you should die and your spouse forgets a monthly loan payment, the trust officer probably can walk down to the loan officer and arrange a grace period until your estate is settled.

5. *Trust management performance.* Since the trustee will be investing your funds, you should inquire about the trustee's track record. Most bank trust departments run their own "common stock funds," which are similar to mutual funds but not open to the general public. You may ask to compare the performance of these funds with mutual funds, the Standard and Poor's "500 Stock Index," or the Dow Jones 30 Industrial Index—just to name a few examples. Be cautious if the trustee is reluctant to discuss investment history with you.

6. *Limitations on investments.* A trust department should not purchase its own securities. A bank trust department should not, for instance, purchase the bank's certificates of deposit or stock. This type of investment is limited by statute in some states. In addition, the trustee must have an investment policy (called the "prudent man" principle). This requires that the trustee buy bonds rated at least "BBB" by Standard and Poor's and rated "Baa" by Moody's Investment Service. Moreover, the department may purchase stocks only rated "A" or better by Standard and Poor's. In fact, the trust department may have even more stringent requirements. Ask about them!

7. *Business operation needs.* If you own a business. you may have a succession plan that will assure the orderly conduct of your business in the event one of the owners dies. Other businesses may not have a person available who can or will manage the business. In these instances, some trustees have competent personnel available to manage the business until the estate is settled or the business is sold. Many trustees do not have such personnel, however. In any event, you should carefully review the trustee's capabilities before establishing a trust, whatever its intended purposes.

8. *Fee structure.* Fees differ among states and among institutions within a state. The fee structure warrants your attention. Fees are discussed in more detail in the following section.

9. *Personnel turnover.* Trust officers can change and may not be with a particular bank or brokerage house when the time comes to manage the trust. You cannot have any real control over this, but you should look for an institution with a history of good personnel and stable employment.

Fee Structure

In most states, the fee structure is established by statute if no reference to fees is made in the will or trust. By way of example, a trust department in the state of New Jersey serving as the executor of your estate would charge 5 percent of the first $200,000 of probate assets, $3\frac{1}{2}$ percent for the next several hundred thousand dollars, and so on. Thus, if your estate had $200,000 of probate assets, the executor's fee in New Jersey would be $10,000. *Probate assets are those passing under the will and do not usually include such outside assets as joint bank accounts, real estate held jointly by spouses with right of survivorship, insurance proceeds with your spouse as beneficiary, pension and profit-sharing plans, and the like.*

It may be that an estate—even quite a large one—consists entirely of outside assets which pass outside probate. In such instances, the executor would still charge a fee, since considerable work may be involved in setting up the estate. The trustee need not be designated as the executor but might perform work for the executor and be compensated for these services on a negotiated basis. A beneficiary, other trusted party, or your lawyer could be named as executor. Using a lawyer as executor will be discussed in more detail in a later section.

Once the estate is settled, the trustee will charge a fee to manage the trust's assets. Using the example of New Jersey again, the typical annual fees are based on the market value of the assets in the trust: 0.5 percent on the first $100,000 of assets in the trust, 0.3 percent on the next $100,000, and 0.2 percent on the remainder. In addition, monthly fees are charged at the rate of 6 percent of the income collected.

Therefore, if a trust had assets with a market value of $100,000 and produced income amounting to $10,000 over the course of the year, the fee would be $1,100 for the year (0.5 percent of $100,000 + 6 percent of $10,000). Income includes interest and dividends. Capital gains and losses, when realized, are not generally considered to be income for purposes of establishing the trustee's fee. Such gains or losses, however, would affect the tax liability of both the trust and the beneficiary. In this situation, *the fees would not vary with the level of activity of the account.* Little incentive therefore exists for the trustee to "churn" the assets.

The fee structure obviously can be an incentive to the trustee. If the estate grows, both the trustee and the beneficiary benefit from increased assets and income. To the extent that the trust is invested in taxable securities, the trustee's fee is tax deductible for income tax purposes.

If the trustee is involved in paying bills for the beneficiary, such as rent, utilities, medical, estimated income tax and the like, the trustee may charge for this service. Usually the fee is minimal, typically $1.00 per transaction. Many trustees do not charge at all. You should discuss fees for these services with the trustee prior to establishing the trust agreement. Some trustees may charge for such "extraordinary services" as hiring nurses for patient care, which may involve the payment of wages and associated record keeping.

Frequently, the trustee will not want to adhere to the statutory fee structure. In this instance, the trustee would request that the trust document include such a statement as, "The fee shall be in effect from time to time . . . ". In such instances, you would want to know the current fees, together with the history of changes and any future fee projections, before deciding upon a particular institution to serve as your trustee. In many instances you may find that fee schedules are actually lower than statutory fees.

INVESTMENT INSTRUCTIONS IN YOUR TRUST?

When establishing a trust, you may specify how you want the money invested and if you will allow distribution of principal. For example, you could direct the trustee to invest the trust's assets in mortgages, utility stocks, bonds, and so on. Some advisors question the appropriateness of such specifications, including the placing of limitations on principal withdrawal by beneficiaries.

Certainly you want the trust to be well managed, but things change over time. Mortgages were great at one time, but if a trust made 30 years ago had stipulated only mortgages, the return today probably would be low. Imagine a trust consisting of mortgages which earn only 5 to 8 percent!

As noted previously, trustees are subject to the "prudent man" standard in making investments. In other words, they are required to exercise the same degree of caution a "prudent man" would exercise in investing other people's funds. *We favor giving the trustee very broad discretion in the choice of assets, realizing that the trustee is required to act prudently in choosing these investments.*

Our recommendation is to give the trustee the discretion to invest funds within the overall objectives of the account. *Furthermore, within prudent limits, we recommend permitting the trustee to distribute principal.* Normally, the trustee would meet with the beneficiary at least once a year to discuss current and future needs for income. Based on the beneficiary's needs, the trustee would invest the account's assets to achieve income, build principal, or retain principal.

The trustee would explain to the beneficiary the importance of maintaining principal and/or building it in order to retain purchasing power in times of inflation. Initially, the surviving spouse may want as much income as possible, since he or she won't know what exact expenses will be. After a year or so, when income needs can be more precisely determined, any income not needed might be reinvested to achieve greater appreciation of assets, unless, of course, the trust requires that all income be distributed.

Normally, transaction statements are sent to the beneficiary every three months—sometimes monthly. These show income generated, investments, stock splits or dividends, fees charged, income distributed to the beneficiary, and bills paid for the beneficiary, if any. These statements may also show a listing of all trust assets, setting forth market values adjusted to the end of the month. Annually, the trustee would provide a detailed statement of assets, including the amount paid for assets, the current market value of the assets, the projected annual income and current yield (a percent figure) for each security, and the percentage of the assets invested in stocks and bonds. These reports provide a sound basis for discussion and formulation of investment decisions by a trustee and the beneficiary.

Finally, the surviving spouse is usually given the right to change the trustee and to appoint another institution as trustee. This gives him or her added flexibility in estate planning

MANAGEMENT OF YOUR TRUST

Institutional trust officers may have some advantages over an individual in managing the account's assets. First, the officer would take into consideration the beneficiary's tax situation in deciding the proportion of the estate to invest in taxable versus nontaxable assets. Second, trust departments do receive discounts on brokerage fees, which are passed along to the trust. Third, the trust officer is in a position to receive the best investment advice from various sources. If you lack faith in the trust officer's ability to make investment decisions, you might want to name a co-trustee (a beneficiary, perhaps) who would approve any changes in the portfolio.

Sound investment of assets is not the only reason to establish a trust. Timely payment of bills, record keeping, transaction reporting—these are other important reasons to have a trust. You or your beneficiary could instruct the trustee to pay all household and other bills (taxes, mortgages, utilities, rent, nursing care, college tuition). Regular, timely payment of such bills obviously could become a real burden on a beneficiary, especially if illness should strike. Having a trust handle this expense makes good sense and is not expensive.

TRUSTEE OR BENEFICIARY AS EXECUTOR?

Someone must be designated executor of your estate. As we said earlier, a trustee would charge an executor's fee. So would a lawyer or other third party. Normally, a fee would not be charged if your primary, or only, beneficiary serves as executor or executrix, since a fee would represent taxable income to both the estate and the beneficiary. Regardless of who serves as executor or executrix, remember that the services of a lawyer, trust department, or other professional person still would be needed.

When a spouse is designated executor or executrix, many bank trust departments would accept appointments as "agent for the executrix." In this capacity, the trust department acts in an advisory rather than in the "partnership" role characteristic of an executor. Any legal, investment, or other services would have to be obtained by the executor or executrix.

If you or your spouse is named executor or executrix, and a large estate is involved, we recommend that you retain a trust department for settlement and estate administration, even though an attorney may be involved. A trust department normally would provide a complete and competent administration of the estate. We cannot always be sure of this if only an attorney is involved, unless he or she is a specialist in estates. In the long run, it may be cheaper to utilize a trust department (and a lawyer of record, if necessary) rather than only an attorney.

If an estate is large or complex, or if a business is involved, a *trustee or lawyer specializing in estates may have a real advantage as executor over your spouse or other beneficiary.* Complicated legal and administrative forms for tax preparation, securities handling, and the like require professional expertise. Moreover, if family members, partners, or shareholders are involved in an estate, you or your spouse serving as executor may be forced to make hard decisions which could affect relatives and friends for a long time. For example, a business may be sold to other shareholders or partners. Unless a buyout agreement clearly spells out the price, your spouse might be asked to sell at a price well below market value. Your spouse may not have the knowledge or objectivity to carry out a complex business transaction in a manner that would serve the interests of the beneficiaries.

SELECTING A LAWYER

A trust document cannot be prepared by a trust department. A lawyer is required. In our opinion, *the best lawyer for this task is one who specializes in trusts*. When you visit trust departments, ask them for the names of lawyers whom they feel are competent in estate planning and trusts.

Your present lawyer may be willing to prepare a trust, but unless he or she is part of a large law firm specializing in the area, you should seek out a specialist. Although some small law firms specialize in trust and estate planning, this normally is not the case. Many attorneys know how to prepare a simple will, but a particularly complex one may require a specialist.

As we pointed out, the cost of a legal specialist may be less in the long run, even though the hourly rate for specialists is considerably more than for "general practitioners." Since portions of the trust document are "boiler plate" (standard statements), these parts of the trust and other common provisions frequently are stored in a word processor—an inexpensive way to prepare documents. Look for a lawyer who utilizes one. Also look for a lawyer who specializes in taxes or has tax specialists on the staff.

Today many people are interviewing attorneys before making a final selection. A lawyer should be willing to spend time talking with potential clients. The client should not be afraid to ask about a lawyer's particular expertise and the firm's experience in dealing with such procedures as billing or general approaches to situations. This information is especially important in dealing with estates.

Once an attorney has been chosen, be sure that this person sends a copy of the preliminary draft of the trust agreement to the trustee for review. You then should plan to meet with the trustee to discuss the details of the document. Once the document is completed, you should plan to review it at least every five years to assure that it meets your current needs.

Selection of an attorney to act as executor or to assist in the administration of your estate also should be made with care. If an attorney is retained, we recommend that you consider the one who prepared your trust document. *Incidentally, in the administration of an estate. the attorney should be willing to agree that fees would be based upon the actual time spent and not upon a percentage of the estate.*

We would be very wary of any attorney who places his or her name in a will, either as executor, trustee, or counsel without being specifically asked. Any attorney who suggests that he or she serve in any of these capacities is suspect. Abusive practices exist in this area, so be careful!

LET'S SUM UP

If you have followed our suggestions, you should be well on your way toward becoming your own best financial advisor—and enjoying financial independence as well. You own or are purchasing a home, your insurance plan provides needed coverage at minimum cost, you have a good credit rating and a "rainy day account," you are saving and investing regularly, and your estate planning is complete.

You will want to monitor your progress regularly—at least every six months and when your situation changes (job changes, a move, new baby). Also, take advantage of the wealth of free information on investments and investment analysis available to you from your public library. Read Chapter 9 to acquaint yourself with these valuable resources. Ongoing study will help you continue to realize your goal of becoming financially independent.

9

BUILDING YOUR KNOWLEDGE POWER

"If you wish success in life, make perseverance your bosom friend, experience your wise counsellor, caution your elder brother and hope your guardian genius."

joseph addison

We have stressed throughout this book that achieving financial independence requires *planning*. Planning, in turn, requires that you know something about the choices available to you and when to take advantage of them. Knowledge is key to becoming your own best financial advisor. Particularly in today's fast-paced world, your success in achieving financial independence depends to a significant degree on keeping abreast of the changing world of finance and economics. We certainly aren't suggesting that you need an MBA or even formal training to become financially knowledgeable. But you will put yourself in the best possible position if you take the time to do a little homework. Often the difference between the successful and unsuccessful investor is that the successful investor knew when to sell what the unsuccessful investor wanted to buy.

The key is knowledge—the kind of knowledge that you can gain from careful observation and study. You've probably known someone who has the "Midas touch" when it comes to investments. What on the surface may look simply like "golden luck" actually is the powerful teaming of knowledge with experience. It's truly a winning combination in financial management.

AN INTRODUCTION TO THE MODERN LIBRARY

Becoming knowledgeable about the world of personal finance involves a little more than just reading the financial page of the daily newspaper or watching the network news programs, such as "Wall Street Week" and the "Nightly Business Report"—useful though these indeed may be. You need to be aware of a number of *key resources* if you are to develop a broad and meaningful base of financial knowledge.

The important thing to remember in building your "knowledge power" is to *develop a consistent plan,* just as it is in financial planning itself. You obviously have only a limited amount of time available to spend on research and study. Use it wisely. *Develop a basic reading list of key books, magazines, journals, and other printed guides and resources.* Then by scanning these key resources regularly, you can learn to spot the trends and developments that will shape your choices.

Where can you find the materials for such a reading list? Visit your public or local college library. Many people do not realize what a treasure house of materials are stored in their neighborhood or regional libraries. Yes, everyone knows that the latest "best seller" can be checked out there. But that's only the "cover on the book."

Let's take a brief tour through the library and point out the major areas that you should be familiar with. Then we can develop a basic reading list. First, we should point out that libraries today are very different from what they were only a few years ago. Most people understandably tend to think of the library as one large bookcase. Nothing could be less accurate! The modern library is an *information center,* with computer terminals linking sister libraries together in a vast regional, state, and even worldwide network. Even though your small-town public library may lack some of these electronic facilities, you can find them in almost any of the larger regional or county public libraries and in many, if not most, college and university libraries. We'll discuss the "electronic library" a little later.

Almost every library, large or small, contains a *basic reference collection* and a *periodicals (or magazine) collection.* The larger the library, of course, the more comprehensive the collections will be. In the reference collection you'll find encyclopedias, directories, almanacs, guidebooks, atlases, dictionaries, tables, charts, and any other book material that contains information that you need to answer specific questions about a particular subject. What's a debenture? What is the currency unit in Switzerland? These are questions that can be answered in the reference collection.

Another major component of any library is the *magazine collection,* or, as it is better termed, the periodicals collection. The larger libraries may subscribe to several thousand titles; the smaller ones maybe only a few dozen. But whatever the size, the library typically subscribes to more than just the newsweekly magazines. Chances are you'll find a variety of specialized journals and magazines representing a wide variety of subjects. In addition, you often can find newsletters, pamphlets, and brochures.

When it comes to periodicals, even the smaller libraries are at no real disadvantage over the bigger libraries. If your library doesn't have a particular subscription, the librarian usually can obtain a photocopy of an article (not the whole magazine) from a library that does have a subscription. This is called *interlibrary loan,* a service that covers not only periodicals but books and other materials as well. Libraries have union lists (compilations of each other's holdings) of periodicals, so it is easy to find out what library has a particular subscription. Furthermore, if you make a request, the library may be willing to add subscriptions and books you want.

But how do you know what article to look for? *All materials housed in a library are indexed.* For books, the most common indexing system is the familiar set of wood card catalogs containing author, title, and subject entry cards for each book the library has. In the case of periodicals, *separate printed indexes* are available for almost every subject area (not every library would subscribe to all the indexes that are published, of course). The most familiar periodicals index is the *Reader's Guide to Periodical Literature,* which gives a subject breakdown of the individual articles, their authors, and where they're located. Other familiar indexes are the *General Science Index,* the *Business Periodicals Index,* and the *Social Sciences Index.*

Today many libraries are taking advantage of computer technology, especially in the area of periodicals. Indexing systems using laser discs provide almost instantaneous retrieval of articles on almost any subject entered on the keyboard. Moreover, many libraries are using computer linkups for buying, processing, and borrowing books. Truly the modern library is more than just four walls: What you get is more than what you see!

Another potentially useful library service we should mention is called *bibliographic database searching.* Many college and university libraries provide access to the many hundreds of information databases available on almost any subject. For example, if you wanted to find detailed information about the history of a particular company that went out of business ten years ago, you might want to ask the librarian to perform a database search for you. For a fee, the librarian can search databases in the business field to try to locate information about your topic. You would then receive a printout listing the titles, authors, subjects, and publications.

GOVERNMENT PUBLICATIONS— A CORNUCOPIA OF FREE INFORMATION

Perhaps you might be surprised to learn that one of the world's largest publishers is not a commercial publisher. The United States Government Printing Office is, in fact, a giant in publishing. What's more, the publications are available in certain "depository libraries" free of charge. On a smaller but no less important scale, state and local governments also publish reports on their activities.

What is a Government Publication?

It may be a report of a congressional hearing, statistics on poverty and welfare, toxic waste studies, airline safety regulations—the list goes on and on. Obviously, the federal and state governments play a large part in our daily lives, from protecting public health to regulating commerce and industry. All the proceedings of federal, state, and many local government conferences, panels, and committees are faithfully recorded and distributed free of charge to depository libraries.

U.S. government publications are indexed in the *Monthly Catalog*. When you locate an item of interest in the catalog, you retrieve it by using the "SUDOC Number" (the Superintendent of Documents Number). Your librarian will help you find what you want. Just ask.

BOOKS, BOOKS, BOOKS

Of course, we haven't forgotten perhaps the largest component of the library: the books. You may not be aware that most libraries can borrow books from other libraries through interlibrary loan. You may be charged a fee for the service, but it probably will be much less than the purchase price.

One useful way to extract more information out of a book is to look at the bibliography—the listing of reference resources at the end of the book. This will give you clues in your search for more information.

THE HOME COMPUTER—A LIBRARY ON YOUR SCREEN

At this point it would be appropriate to mention the important new role of the home computer in information retrieval. Over the past several years, the home computer has become almost as common as the vacuum cleaner or the microwave oven. If you have any one of the popular brands of home computer and a modem, you can access *information utilities*. These are companies that provide a variety of information, education, and entertainment services on-line. *Compuserve* and *The Source* are two of the major information utilities. Other more specialized services also are available.

Particularly germane to this book, the home-computer information utilities provide on-line information on business and investment. *The Source* and *Compuserve,* for example, provide stock and bond price quotes, historical analysis, currency reports, as well as a securities portfolio program for monitoring your own investments. Another information utility, *Bibliographic Research Services,* offers "BRS after Dark," a lower-cost access to information databases in many different subjects.

A word of caution. Knowledge indeed is power, but knowledge is not cheap. On-line computer time is expensive. If you are a serious investor who wants up-to-date information with a minimum of "legwork," home computer information retrieval may be the answer. But for most of us, a trip to the public or college library can provide us with all the current resources we need.

DEVELOPING A BASIC LIST OF READING MATERIALS

"Nothing can beat the insight of hindsight."

Now that we have taken a brief tour of what's available in the library and on the home computer, let's begin to put together a basic list of resources to help you become knowledgeable about financial opportunities.

I. Home Mortgages and Real Estate

The following are recommended U.S. Government publications, available from the U.S. Dept. of Housing and Urban Development, 451 Seventh Street, SW, Washington, DC 20410:

1. *Questions and Answers on FHA Home Property* (HUD-38-H.)
2. *Financing Condominium Housing* (HUD-77-H.)
3. *Let's Consider Cooperatives* (HUD-17-H.)
4. *Home Mortgage Insurance* (HUD-43-F.)
5. *HUD's Home Ownership Subsidy Program* (HUD-419.)
6. *Protecting Your Housing Investment* (HUD-346-PA.)
7. *Home Owner's Glossary of Building Terms* (HUD-369-H.)

The following are recommended books:

1. *Income Property Mortgage Servicing Handbook,* 1983, Mortgage Bankers.
2. McClean, Andrew J. *The Complete Guide to Real Estate Loans,* 1983, Contemporary Books.
3. Reid, Charles F. *Illustrated Guide to Residential Financing,* 1984, Paine-Webber Mortgage.

II. Insurance

The following are recommended books:

1. *Insurance,* The Changing Times Education Service Editors, 1982, EMC.
2. Kennedy, David W. *Insurance, What Do You Need? How Much Is Enough?* 1987, HP Books.
3. Sundheim, Finn A. *How to Insure a Business: Solving the Insurance Business Puzzle,* 1983, Venture Publications.

III. Retirement and Estate Planning

The following are recommended books:

1. Hoffman, Ray. *Extra Dollars: Easy Money-Making for Retired People,* 1977, Stein and Day.
2. Page, Cynthia L., ed. *Your Retirement: How to Plan for a Secure Future,* 1984, ARCO.
3. Sloan, Leonard. *The New York Times Book of Personal Finance,* 1985, Times Books.
4. Vicker, Ray. *The Dow Jones-Irwin Guide to Retirement Planning,* 1985, Dow Jones-Irwin.
5. Weaver, Peter, and Buchanan, Annette. *What to Do with What You've Got: The Practical Guide to Money Management in Retirement,* 1987, American Association of Retired Persons.

IV. Investments

The following books and reference works are recommended:

1. *Barrons* (Weekly Financial Newspaper).
2. *Disclosure* (SEC 10-K and 10-Q Filing Reports).

Developing a Basic List of Reading Materials

3. *Mutual Fund Forecaster* (Newsletter), Institute for Econometric Research, Ft. Lauderdale, FL 33306.
4. Standard and Poor's. *Industry Surveys* and *Stock Reports*.
5. Moody's Investment Service. *Moody's Manuals* for banking and finance and industry.
6. *Value Line Investment Survey.*
7. *The Wall Street Journal.*

The following government publications are recommended:

1. *Business Statistics,* U.S. Dept. of Commerce.
2. *Social Indicators,* U.S. Office of Federal Statistical Policy.
3. *Survey of Current Business,* U.S. Dept. of Commerce.
4. *U.S. Industrial Outlook,* U.S. Dept. of Commerce.

V. Financing a College Education

The following pamplet is recommended:

1. "The Student Guide: Five Federal Financial Aid Programs 86–87," U.S. Department of Education, 400 Maryland Ave., SW, Washington, DC 20202.

The following books are recommended:

1. *The College Cost Book,* 1986–87, The College Board.
2. Brownstone, David M., and Hawes, Gene R. *The College Money Book: How to Get a High-Quality Education at the Lowest Possible Cost,* 1984, Bobbs.
3. Hegener, Karen C., ed. *The College Money Handbook,* 1986, AMS Press.
4. Lane, Paul. *Dow Jones-Irwin Guide to College Financial Planning,* 1983, Dow Jones-Irwin.

VI. Your Own Business

We recommend checking with the trade association which supports the particular business you are considering. Trade associations can provide valuable information in starting and operating a business. Check *The Encyclopedia of Associations* (Gale Publications) in your library for addresses.

You may want to consider the following books:

1. Osgood, William R. *Basics of Successful Business Planning,* 1982, AMACOM.
2. Klug, John R. *The Complete Guide to Running a Business.* 1983, Boardroom.
3. Maier, Daniel W. *The Complete Guide to Starting your Own Business,* 1983, Moneymatters.
4. Leza, Richard, and Placenia, Jose. *Develop your Business Plan,* 1982, PSI Research.
5. Clark, Leta W. *How to Open Your Own Shop or Gallery,* 1980, Penguin.
6. Delany, W. *How to Run a Growing Company,* 1983, AMACOM.
7. Armstrong, A. W. *How to Use Lotus 1-2-3 for Productive Business Applications,* 1985, Wiley.
8. Jessup, Claudia, and Chipps, Genie. *The Woman's Guide to Starting a Business,* 1980, Harper & Row.

TRACKING THE PERIODICALS

The books mentioned above represent only a small fraction of the universe of library material available on personal financial management. In addition to these books, we encourage you to read some of the important magazines and journals that relate to our topic:

- *Business Week*
- *Changing Times*
- *Forbes*
- *Consumer Reports*
- *Fortune*
- *Harvard Business Review*
- *Inc.*
- *Money*
- *Moneysworth*

If you are interested in pursuing any topic at greater depth, check the *Standard Periodicals Directory* in your library for a listing of magazines and journals.

LET'S SUM UP

Your library can become a powerful partner in your program to develop financial independence. Even the smaller libraries have access to a wealth of materials in all aspects of personal financial management. Thanks to computer technology, the modern library can provide access to a large number of databases in which you can find the latest information on almost any subject.

But to use the library efficiently and effectively, you must have a plan for your research. By developing the habit of reading selected materials on a regular basis, you will gain important insights into the changing world of finance, banking, real estate, running your own business and investments. Good luck!

Index

Acid test, 125
Adjustable rate mortgage, 38–39
A. M. Best Co., 67
American Society of Appraisers, 56
Annual Percentage Rate (APR), 9, 18
Assessed valuation, 28
Automobile financing:
    leasing, 111–13
    reducing payments, 110–11
Automobile insurance, 60–61

Barrons, 121
Bibliographical Research Services, 177
Bonds:
    call feature, 87–88
    corporate, 76, 87–88
    municipal, 133–36
    ratings, 87, 163
    Series EE, 76, 80–83, 107
    Series HH, 76, 82
    U.S. Treasury, 76, 83–84
    zero coupon, 88
Business investments (*see* Owning your own business)

Call option, 129
Certificates of deposit (CDs), 75, 78–79
Checking account, 5
    service charges, 5
Collectibles, 76
College education, funding, 107–9
    creative financing, 107–8
    Series EE bonds, 107
    Uniform Gift to Minors Account, 107
Commodities, 76
Common stock, 7, 86–87
    accumulation trading pattern, 128
    analysis, 119–29
    Beta, 125
    book value, 127

Common stock (*continued*)
  chartists, 128
  covered call option writing, 129–33
  distribution trading pattern, 129
  dividend policy, 125
  earnings growth, 127
  fundamental analysis, 122–24
  insider trading, 127
  liquidity, 125
  market value, 127–28
  net profit margin, 126
  price/earnings ratio, 124
  return on equity, 126
  risk assessment, 119–21
  technical analysis, 122
  volatility, 124–25
  volume trends, 128
Compuserve, 177
Condominiums, 25
Contingency planning, 109–10
Conventional mortgages, 34
Corporate securities, 76, 86–89
Covered call option writing, 125, 129–33
  calculating return, 131–32
  full-move rate of return, 131
  static rate of return, 131
  strike price, 130
Credit cards, 6
  insurance, 57
  yearly fee, 7
Credit history, 6
Credit report, 41

Data base search, 175
Deductibles, insurance, 51
Discount points, 34
Dun & Bradstreet, 126

Electronic funds transfer, 6
Employer benefits, 8
  disability insurance, 9
  educational, 9
  life insurance, 9
Equalization ratios, 28
Estate planning, 155–69
  selecting a lawyer, 168–69
  trusts, 157, 160–68
  wills, 158–60

"Fannie Maes," 85–86
Federal Housing Administration (FHA) mortgages, 35–36
Financial goals and planning:
  contingency planning, 109–10
  establishing goals, 13, 18–19, 75
  estate planning, 155–69
Float, 6
Fringe benefits, employer, 8

"Ginnie Maes," 85–86
Government backed securities, 85–86
Government publications, 175–76
Group life insurance, 52, 62

Home Equity Loans, 10–12, 96
Homeowner's Insurance, 52–55
  appraised replacement value, 56
  computer coverage, 57
  deductibles, 55, 58
  earthquake coverage, 57
  employer's liability, 57
  flood coverage, 57
  full replacement coverage, 53–54
  inventory form, 56
  liability coverage, 57
  loss of use coverage, 57
  proving a loss, 55–56
  replacement cost estimator, 54
  scheduled property, 54, 56
  unscheduled property, 54–56

Index

Home purchasing and ownership:
  advantages, 23–24
  as an investment, 75–76
  assessed valuation, 28
  condominiums, 25, 27
  development homes, new, 26–28
  engineering survey, 32
  financing, 33–37
  handyman's special, 32
  location, 28–29
  mechanical and electrical certification, 32
  Mortgages (*see* Mortgages)
  negotiating a price, 42–43
  repros, 33
  settlement costs, 43–44

Individual Retirement Account (IRA), 9, 99, 103–6
  and CDs, 79, 88
  investment alternatives, 106
  premature withdrawal, 105
  qualification for tax deductibility, 103–4
  severe penalty, 105
  variable interest accounts, 80
  and zero coupon bonds, 88
Inflation, 14–15, 19
Insider trading, 127
Institute of Certified Financial Planners, 122
Insurance:
  automobile (*see* Automobile insurance)
  choosing an agent, 52
  credit card, 57
  deductibles, 51, 58
  discounts, 52
  guide for getting best value, 51–52
  Homeowner's (*see* Homeowner's Insurance)
  life (*see* Life insurance)
  tenant, 57
  umbrella liability, 58, 59–60
Interest:
  compound, 15, 98
  effective rate, 17, 18
  inflation and, 14–15
  mortgage (*see* Mortgages)
  real rate (inflation adjusted), 14
  stated rate, 17
  tax deductibility, 10
Investment information, 173–80
Investments:
  consistency in, 96–97
  core program, 96–113
  discretionary, 119
  diversification, 19, 118
  liquidity, 118
  planning, 18–19
  securities, 117–36

Libraries, 173–80
Life insurance, 61–71
  actual rates of return, 67
  carrier ratings, 67
  determining how much you need, 68–71
  group life, 52, 62, 68
  independent rating service, 67
  mortgage creditor, 29, 64
  nonsmoking discount, 71
  single payment, 66
  Social Security survivor benefits, 99, 103
  surrender value (universal), 66
  tax deferred annuities, 91–92
  term, 62–64, 68
  universal, 65–67
  variable, 67–68
  whole, 65
Location, good for property purchase, 28–29

Market risk, 79, 83, 84, 87, 88
Money magazine, 90
Money management, 5, 75
Money market deposit accounts, 75, 79
Money market mutual funds, 91
Mortgage creditor life insurance, 29
Mortgage insurance premium, 34
Mortgages:
   adjustable rate, 38–39
   advantages of short term, 17
   amortization schedule, 46
   automatic payment, 6
   conventional, 34
   equity in, 23
   Federal Housing Administration (FHA), 35–36
   fees (origination, processing, funding), 34
   graduated payment, 37
   interest rate, factors affecting, 34–35
   monthly payment, determining, 29
   negotiating rates, 40–41
   payments, calculation of, 29–31
   period, 37–38
   points, 34–36
   prepayment, 44–45, 95, 97–98
   principal, 23
   qualifying for, 29–32
   refinancing, 44
   reverse, 25
   seller held, 36
   Veterans Administration, 36
Municipal bonds, 76, 133–36
   analysis, 134–35
   general obligation bonds, 135
   ratings, 135
   revenue bonds, 135
Municipal Bond Unit Trusts, 76, 135–36

Mutual funds, 77, 89–91, 123
   load, 80
   money market, 91
   no load, 80
   ratings, 90
   "12(b)" fee, 80

National Insurance Consumer Organization (NICO), 67
Negotiable Order of Withdrawal (NOW) Account, 5, 78

Owning your own business, 139–41
   profiting from a hobby, 142
   tax advantages, 140–41

Passbook savings accounts, 75, 78
Payroll deductions, 7
Pension plans:
   employer-provided, 98–102
   tax deferred, 8
   vesting benefits, 100
Periodicals collections, 174–75
Points, 34
Power of attorney, 7
Preferred stock, 76, 89
Prepaying a mortgage, 44–47
Private mortgage insurance, 34
Property elevation certificate, 57
"Prudent man" principle, 163

Rainy day account, 7, 95, 96
Real estate, investment, 143–52
   financial incentives, 24
   financial leverage, 76
   leases, 149–50
   property management, 145–47
   purchasing rental property, 147–49
   risk, 120–23

Index

security deposits, 151
selecting tenants, 150–52
Refinancing a mortgage, 44
Registered Investment Advisor, 122
Retirement planning, 95, 98–103
Risk:
  default, 77, 83, 84, 87, 88
  market, 79, 83, 84, 87, 88
Robert Morris Statement Studies, 126

Series EE bonds, 76, 80–83
  and college savings, 107
  payroll deduction plans, 81
Series HH bonds, 76, 82
Settlement costs, home purchase, 43–44
Social Security retirement benefits, 99–100
Social Security survivor benefits, 69
Statement savings accounts, 75, 78
Stock (*See* Common stock; Preferred stock)
Stock repurchase plans, 127
Source, The, 177

Tax deferred annuities, 77, 91–92 (*see also* **Life insurance**)
Tax rates:
  average, 134
  marginal, 134
Tax Reform Act of 1986, 10, 26, 82, 101, 108, 125, 145
Term life insurance, 62–64
Treasury bills, 76, 83, 126
Treasury bonds, 76, 83–84, 87
Treasury notes, 76
Trusts, 160–68

Umbrella liability insurance, 58, 59–60
Uniform Gift to Minors Account, 82, 107–9
Universal life insurance, 65–67

Variable life insurance, 67–68
Veterans Administration mortgage, 36

Whole life insurance, 65
Wills, 158–60

Zero coupon bonds, 88